I just wanted to tell you that I am a Radio Announcer on my own radio show, "Country Mornings With Karen Kelly" - WBKI in Ohio. I use your e-mails daily as my OWN inspiration to help me inspire other people - my listeners! So THANK YOU! Through you, I am helping thousands feel good about themselves every morning!
Sincerely, Karen Kelly

Just want to say thank you, MountainWings. My husband and I just opened a "Mom and Pop" restaurant and to help customers pass time while waiting for their food, I have printed off some of your stories. Not only are they enjoying them, they are asking if they can take them with them. You are making a difference.

My husband lost his job, I am losing my job. He now has a new and better job and I know I will have one also. Part of the positive attitude we have maintained is due to the enlightening and positive messages found daily in MountainWings.

I really enjoy all of the MountainWings I have been receiving, they really lift me up. I can hardly wait until the next MountainWings comes tomorrow.
I really appreciate them. Thank You very much!!!

I have been on the internet about one month and have a lot to learn, but thank God, I found MountainWings.com. It is such a fresh breath of air, with gentle words and deep wisdom. It now goes hand-in-hand with my morning cup of coffee. I would not want to do without it.
It inspires my thoughts and brings me smiles, and generally helps me to make my emotional life peaceful.

DOES GOD E-MAIL? (subject in an e-mail to MountainWings)
Something really weird happened to me just now.
I'm having some marital difficulties and I was writing my wife an e-mail. The e-mail turned really ugly and was really negative, pointing out all the bad and none of the good. Then I got an e-mail from MountainWings about a man and a bum and the bum makes the man realize that we all need something. I have been looking for "something" all my life and people keep telling me about God.

Until now it has fallen on deaf ears but something about your e-mail and it's timing, it was too perfect to be coincidence. I have no idea who sent my name or knew that I was in need of inspiration. I scrapped the negative e-mail and wrote an apology instead.

For a long time, I have felt the need to let God into my life. I've been fighting it though and now I'm feeling ready to let Him in. Please pray for me being successful in letting God into my life because I am scared.
Thank you so much.

I run internet businesses and daily my mailbox is overflowing with offers, business ideas, scams and schemes. Today a friend from New Mexico sent me a copy of MountainWings and while this isn't the first time I've seen isolated inspirational messages, it is the first time that I've found a daily dose to remind me that life should be so much more than that headlong pursuit of making a buck.

Don't get me wrong...we all need that too, but its nice during a hectic business day to just pause and contemplate that life holds so much more.
Warmest Regards and Thanks E. N., Sydney Australia

MountainWings
Moments
Parables of Life

112 Stories to Help You
Over The Mountains of Life

Original stories from
MountainWings.com

The daily e-mail read by
over a million people

MountainWings
Atlanta Ga USA

All stories except as noted are written by Nathaniel Bronner Jr. For a bio on the author, go to QuickFasting.com and click, "This Is Me."

MountainWings wishes to thank the subscribers of MountainWings for their inspiration, support, encouragement, and constant requests for a book.

May this book bless you...then pass the blessing on. For when you pass it on, it shall return to you ...blessed and multiplied.

Many thanks also to those who helped in the production of Parables of Life:

MountainWings logo: Bill Leavell billleavell.com
Cover design: Ithan Payne   artbyidesign.com
Proofreading: Britte Blair
Typesetting, layout, and photos: Shelli Barnes
Website technical assistance: James Bronner
Graphics coordinator and retouch:
        Gary Crawford   crawfordadvertising.com
MountainWings Advice Requests Counselor:
        Dr. E. T. Shorter
Additional authors:
        C. Elijah Bronner
        Dr. Dale C. Bronner
        James Bronner
        Britte Blair
        MountainWings subscribers as indicated,
        many of whom choose to remain anonymous

*and foremost praise to the Divine Creator,
the source of all inspiration - It's Amazing!*

MountainWings Moments

Welcome to MountainWings

Prepare to Fly!

MountainWings
120 Selig Dr.
Atlanta, Ga 30336
www.mountainwings.com
books@mountainwings.com

ISBN 0-9725818-0-4 (hardcover)
ISBN 0-9725818-1-2 (paperback)

Hi, my name is Dora Justice.

I had been going through a hard time.
I was sitting on my porch and just asked,

"Why am I going through so much?"

A small voice spoke in my mind and said,
"To whom much is given."

I thought I had heard or read that sentence somewhere
even though it was not complete.

Then I got MountainWings and read the e-mail.
To my surprise, it was identical
to what had happened to me.

Thanks so much for sending it to me.

The Bum
=======

"You can easily judge the character of a man by how he treats those who can do nothing for him."
-James D. Miles

Everyone respects and helps the millionaire, the famous, the boss, those with beauty and brains.

What about the bum on the street?

This is a real story. It happened to me, the writer of MountainWings.com.

I was parked in front of the church cleaning out my Jeep. I was waiting on someone.

Coming my way from across the street was what society would consider a bum.

From the looks of him, he had no car, no home, no clean clothes, and no money.

There are times when you feel generous, but there are other times when you just don't want to be bothered.

This was one of those "don't want to be bothered times."

"I hope he doesn't ask me for any money," I thought.

He didn't.

He came and sat on the wall in front of the bus stop to wait on the bus.

After a few minutes he spoke.

"That's a very pretty Jeep," he said.

He was ragged, but he had an air of dignity around him.

His scraggly blond beard kept more than his face warm. I said, "thanks," and continued cleaning out the Jeep.

He sat there quietly as I worked. The expected plea for money never came.

As the silence between us widened, something inside said, "ask him if he needs any help."

I was sure that he would say yes, but I held true to the inner voice.

"Do you need any help?" I asked.

He answered in three simple but profound words that I shall never forget.

We often look for wisdom in great men and women. We expect it from those of higher learning and accomplishments.

I expected nothing but an outstretched grimy hand.

He spoke the three words that shook me.

"Don't we all?" he said.

I was feeling high and mighty, successful and important, above a bum in the street, until those three words hit me like a twelve gauge shotgun.

Don't we all?

I needed help. Maybe not for bus fare or a place to sleep, but I needed help.

I reached in my wallet and gave him not only enough for bus fare, but enough to take a cab anywhere in the city and get food and shelter for the day.

Those three little words still ring true.

No matter how much you have, no matter how much you have accomplished, you need help too.

No matter how little you have, no matter how loaded you are with problems, even without money or a place to sleep, you can give help.

Even if it's just a compliment, you can give that.

You never know when you may see someone who appears to have it all. They are waiting on you to give them what they don't have.

A different perspective on life, a glimpse at something beautiful, a respite from daily chaos, that only you through a torn world can see.

Maybe the man was just a homeless stranger wandering the streets.

Maybe he was more than that.
Maybe he was sent by a power that is great and wise, to minister to souls too comfortable in themselves.

Maybe God looked down, called an angel, dressed him like a bum, then said, "go minister to that man cleaning the Jeep, that man needs help."

Don't we all?

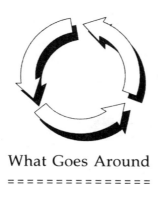

What Goes Around
===============

I received a forwarded issue of MountainWings.

I thought that was ironic. Here it is that I write
MountainWings and someone forwards me an issue.

Evidently, they didn't know that I write MountainWings.
As you may have noticed, I don't put my name on any of
the issues; most of you don't even know my name.
My name isn't important, your daily climb is.

So, I received this issue of MountainWings from someone
who obviously didn't know that I wrote the thing.

What goes around comes around.

I read the issue. . . again.

It blessed me.

I don't believe that you receive back what you send out.

I believe you send out seeds and receive back fruit.

You receive back what you send out, with interest.

The longer I live, the more I believe, see, and understand this principle.

It may be delayed, but it's coming back.

I've seen the seeds parents sow come back through their children, good or bad.

It may be delayed, but it's coming back.

I've seen the seeds of the spirit that people sow come back in their bodies, lives, and relationships, good or bad.

It may be delayed, but it's coming back.

I've seen the seeds of financial spending or saving that people sow come back.

It may be delayed, but it's coming back.

I don't know through what routers, ISP's, and internet backbones that issue of MountainWings went through. It stopped for a while then traveled at nearly the speed of light, but it came back.

Just like everything else, that which you plant, you will harvest. It may be delayed, but it's coming back, not just the seeds, but the fruit.

It's coming back!

Plant Wisely!

You Will Meet Them Too

===================

MountainWings.com has a lot of subscribers in over 2,000 cities and 125 countries. The vast majority is silent and our email is flooded each day with testimonies how MountainWings has changed lives for the better.

Approximately one in every few thousand is totally obnoxious and vulgar. They will write and the e-mail will be loaded with curse words and derogatory statements; you name it, they write it. They rudely demand to be removed from the list when all it takes to be removed is about 10 seconds with a quick click to MountainWings.com.

It no longer bothers us, it did at first, but you get used to it. You begin to see the spirit behind it and eventually feel more compassion than anger. They are often hurting very deeply themselves and only know how to lash out as they have been lashed out against.

The reason that I am telling you this is that sooner or later, you will meet them too, just as MountainWings does.

At work, in the family, at the mall, on the golf course, in the gym, at church, or even a faceless foreign enemy, sooner or later you will meet someone who for reasons that have nothing to do with you, will violently lash out at you.

The first temptation when that happens to you is to fight fire with fire. The key to that phrase is "fight." An angry violent person will draw you into a fight, if you let them.

You have three choices when you meet them.

1. Fight - Return blow for blow, an eye for an eye. They curse - you curse, they swing - you swing, they glare - you glare; that's the essence of fighting. In a fight, not only do you return blow for blow, but also you try to get in more blows. You end up trying to out curse, out shout, out glare, and out hate the enemy.

2. Ignore Them - Say nothing, do nothing, become numb to them, and hope they go away.

3. Return Love for Hate - Each of these gets harder to do. Loving your enemy is not an easy thing to do. It goes against every nerve cell in the body and our cultural training.

Jesus told us to do that. I now understand why.

Anger and hate kill, not just the other person, but you.

Anger and hate will raise your blood pressure, irritate your nerves, tense your entire body, and even constipate you.

There is a long list of physical illnesses that are caused by mental stress. Anger and hate lead the list in causing stress just as love leads the list in relieving stress.

I thought Jesus said "Love Your Enemy" to help the other person. It helps the other person, but the greatest benefit is to you.

There was a particularly nasty note from a 12-year-old boy. I was astounded that a 12-year-old would talk that way.

Each time I see a virulent e-mail, I now bow my head and pray for the peace of that person. Hopefully the prayer helps them.

I too have the three choices: I can get mad and respond in the same violent manner; I can ignore it, although it will still burn inside of me like a small flame, or I can pray for the peace of that person.

When I pray for their peace, it brings my peace.
I understand now that loving your enemy is really loving yourself.

Remember this when you meet them, for surely you will.

They will curse and fuss, huff and puff, stare and glare, criticize and taunt you for something that is not your fault.

Remember, it's not you who has caused the real pain; those wounds are more likely from an age long before you.

Learn to pray for them, learn to love them, for surely as you read this, sooner or later, you will meet them.

Be prepared to love them; you need it.

What Would I Do?

===============

"Everything's perfect," Dr. Stewart said.

Dr. Stewart is my wife's doctor. She asked me to come along for her routine checkup. She feels better when I go with her.

Dr. Stewart has been my wife's doctor during the eight years that we have been married.

I looked at Dr. Stewart. He was vibrant, his skin was as smooth as a baby's and his face was radiant. Dr. Stewart actually looked younger than he did eight years ago.

"When are you going to retire?" my wife asked in conversation.

"I'm not going to retire," Dr. Stewart promptly answered without even stopping to think about it.

"What would I do?" he added.

"I've bought and sold several boats; I don't want another one. I don't want a house in the mountains. I have more patients now than I did when I was younger.

I have everything that I want now.

What would I do if I retired?"

After dealing with many in both business and ministry,
I have become more sensitive to real reasons,
the underlying motivation behind the statements.
I understood what he was saying.
I could feel his spirit in that simple question.

"What would I do?"

Most people dread going to work. Dr. Stewart cherishes it.
Most look forward to being able to do nothing.
Dr. Stewart looks forward to another day helping
patients. Most look at the clock counting the minutes
until quitting time. Dr. Stewart wishes there were more
hours in the day.

Being a doctor is not a breeze. Doctors have one of the
highest suicide rates of any profession. It is strenuous
and demanding.

Doctors also have one of the highest rates of personal
satisfaction of any profession; it just depends on the doctor.

Joy always depends much more on the person than the
profession.

Dr. Stewart is happily married with four successful
children. One of his sons is even a doctor in the same
specialty as his father.

For Dr. Stewart, work is not an escape, it is a passion.

There is a big difference.

Passion helps keep you young, in both mind and body. It usually shows on the outside when you have passion on the inside about something good.

To be able to do something each day that you are passionate about is a blessing beyond price.

It is like being paid to play.

The average person spends more time involved with work than anything else. Adding the time at work, getting ready for work, and getting to and from work, we average 12 hours a day.

With eight hours of sleep, we spend 75% of our waking hours for work. What a blessing to WANT to work, even if you didn't have to.

Imagine getting up each morning with an enthusiasm to get to work. Imagine an enthusiasm to get home to your family.

At work and at home, you are fulfilled and have no desire to retire from or change either. So fulfilled that you couldn't imagine wanting anything else.

Imagine that.

That Hill

========

Are you running that hill or is that hill running you?

I was jogging, sweating, and breathing rather hard. I had jogged about 3 miles and I wasn't even halfway yet.

As I was jogging up a hill, a man about my age stood in his front yard watching me run. He stood cool and comfortable as sweat enveloped my body. No rapid breaths came from his lungs.

He looked at me as if to say, "I'm not fool enough to do that in this heat."

He spoke and said rather jokingly,
"Are you running that hill or is that hill running you?"

MountainWings has changed my thought patterns.

So many of you have written and expressed how MountainWings has influenced your lives and thinking. It has changed me too. I now instantly recognize a MountainWings moment. It's a moment in time and circumstance when life gives me an opportunity to fly or flop.

All of us have MountainWings moments each day; this was mine for the day.

Was the hill running me or was I running the hill?

Is the obstacle that you are facing running you or are you running it?

It makes a difference which way you look at it.

I don't like to flop. I prefer to fly. Although said joking-ly, I took the question seriously. I decided I was not going to let any hill run me.

The thing is, the hill doesn't care. The hill will be there, as unmoving and unconcerned as a tired dog watching cars from the porch on a hot day.

Is your utility bill up? That's a hill. Are they putting pressure on you at work? That's a hill. Do you have some mean people in your life? That's a hill. Are you getting older? That's a blessing, though it looks like a hill.

I have decided that no hill is going to run me.

I stepped high and spoke in my mind to the hill, "thanks for the workout, because of you I'm getting a real run that will make me stronger. You may put a strain on me, but I'll be in better shape for you next time. If it wasn't for you, I would be weaker. Besides, in reality, I've got you under my feet."

The hill didn't respond but faded in the distance as my stride lengthened.

Who's in charge of your hill?

The Toy

=======

El and Josees, my 6 and 3-year-old boys, were wailing at the top of their lungs in the back of the van.

Tears were streaming down their cheeks.

"What's wrong?" I asked, not knowing who had upset whom and preparing to try to figure out what would have stumped Sherlock Holmes.

"Josees won't give me the toy, and he played with it already!" EL exclaimed loudly through tears while tugging at the small airplane clasped in Josees' Super Glue grip.

"I had it first!" Josees wailed.

It was not a simple solution. All parents have faced similar situations. Suddenly, I had a brilliant flash of insight.

"I will let whoever stops crying first play with the toy," I said.

I was smug in my wisdom. Here was a solution that would help them consider not crying when they didn't get their way and would allow me to administer some form of justice.

I had not counted on what happened next.

Before I spoke my basis for judgment, the van was a cacophony of sound, each trying to out cry the other.

"I will let whoever stops crying first play with the toy."

DEAD SILENCE

I mean not a peep.

Instantly

...from them both.

There was no basis for rendering judgment because each of them shut up instantly. Not a single whimper escaped. They were both quiet before my words could stop echoing.

I was standing there with my mouth hanging open wondering how two kids could turn crying off so suddenly and completely.

It was a MountainWings Moment.

How much whimpering, whining, complaining, crying, and bellyaching do we do that we can really cut off if we want to?

Maybe we don't have the toy we want.
Maybe someone else has what we want.

So we cry.

I learned a lesson from my sons.

Often if we choose, we can stop the crying.

Instantly.

The Greatest Temptation
====================

What is the greatest temptation that you face?

All of us have temptation, usually on a daily basis.

What is your biggest one?

Success in life involves the ability to overcome temptations. They are everywhere but some are stronger and have greater consequences than others.

Temptations test us. Temptations try us.
Temptations make us stronger if we overcome them.
Temptations often break us when we don't.

What is your greatest temptation?

Is it illicit money; the desire to take what is not yours?
Most of the time it's not outright robbery, it's subtle.
Cheating on your taxes, padding expenses, fudging,
money not paid back, business practices that you know
are not fully honest, walking away when you are given
too much change, and a host of other things that
challenge real honesty.

Is it gossip?
Bad news that someone shared with you in trust.
It burns within for you to just tell ONE person.
Maybe it's something that someone told you or you have
seen, and you just need to tell someone else about it.

Is it food?

That's a big one. When food overcomes us we can't hide it long, it shows up right in the middle.

Is it an intoxicant?

Have weeds and seeds mastered us?

Read Weeds and Seeds, page 375.

Is it the desire for another person?

The grass looks greener on the other side and sometimes it is, but it's not our grass, and that's the point.

Is it pride?

If we master the things of the world, just the extreme feeling of accomplishment is a temptation in itself.

Will I tell you my greatest temptation?

Hardly

It doesn't matter; you've got your own greatest tempta-tion, your own struggles, your own lures, traps and valleys. We all do.

How do you handle temptation, both great and small?

Simple, just turn and walk away.

Those are two separate actions.

First turn.

If you are heading towards the thing, change.

Change your thinking, change your imaginations, and change your focus. Stop focusing on the brief pleasure and see the long-term pain. When we head towards temptation, we always only look at the brief pleasure.

Next, walk away.
Start MOVING in the other direction.

If food is your temptation, don't stand before an open refrigerator fighting temptation. Close the door and walk away.

You will never prove how strong you are by staring real temptation continually in the eye.

You will only prove where your breaking point is.

Simple things are often not easy, but they are simple.

Simply turn and walk away, from your greatest temptation.

You'll be glad you did in the long run.

The Gifts
==========

In my years in ministry, I have never been on salary.
I don't collect a "Love Offering" for myself.
Ministry is something that I do without cost.
There is nothing wrong with being paid as a Pastor.
The Biblical way is to receive some form of support.
For the moment, I simply choose not to.

On father's day last year, a young man came up to me
after church. I did not recognize him. I have not seen
him since. He was in his late teens or early 20s.

As I stood at the front of the church shaking hands, he
approached me and said, "I watch you on TV and I just
want to give you this," as he handed me a piece of paper
rolled up like a cigarette.

I thought it was another appeal for help of some kind or
who knows what. You can get some weird things in
ministry. I thought nothing more about it. I threw the
paper in the back seat of my car along with a myriad of
other papers that I had accumulated.

A week later as I was cleaning out my car, I noticed what
appeared to be a receipt for a money order lying on my
back seat. I looked at it. It said $500.00.

"Who would put a receipt for a $500.00 money order on
my seat?" I thought. I looked at it again, this time more
carefully.

It couldn't be! I checked it again and again.

It wasn't a receipt.

It was a real money order for $500.00.

There was no indication who the money order was from.

I noticed another similar piece of paper still on the seat.

I picked it up.

It was another $500.00 money order. I immediately checked my back seat thoroughly. There was another money order, this one for $300.00.

There was also a note.

On my backseat were three money orders, totaling $1,300.00, and a note.

The note read, "You have been like a father to me."

I stood there scratching my head wondering where in the world did these money orders come from? Did my mother give them to me for father's day and slip them in my car?

I called her and asked. She knew nothing about them.

I asked my wife. She looked at me, perhaps wondering if I had started drinking or something. $1,300.00 of money orders just lying on your back seat?

I looked at the money orders closely. There was absolutely no indication of the origin but then I noticed one thing. All of the money orders had a slight curl. I placed them in a stack.

The curls all fit together neatly, like in a roll, like in a cigarette roll.

I placed the note on top of the money orders. The note had the same curl.

The young man at the church, the rolled up piece of paper, he had given me $1,300.00!

That was by far the largest gift in ministry that I have ever received. It impacted me. It made me also remember never to prejudge anyone, for you know not what they bear.

Months later, another regular attendee of the church gave me an envelope for Christmas.

In it was a card.

In the card was cash money.

It was a worn and faded one-dollar bill.

My first reaction was, "Is this all in this card. . . $1?"

Then I realized, he didn't have to give me that, no one else did. It was all that he could afford. I began to see that worn dollar bill in a new light, a widow's mite.

Those two gifts are the only two that stand out in my mind; the only ones that I really remember. In both instances I misjudged the givers and jumped to wrong conclusions. We are all human and make errors.

Those gifts represent the extremes for me in amounts, but they were given with the same spirit.

I teach here a principle of spirit.

We are sometimes ashamed because we don't have as much as our neighbors or friends. Both the $1,300.00 and the $1.00 had great impact on me. The person who gave the $1.00 was in dire financial straits himself. He didn't have much and virtually none to spare. But he had $1.00, and he gave it.

We must always be careful with our words and declarations.

Never say that you don't have anything. That's not true. If you have the capability to receive MountainWings via e-mail, you are more materially blessed than 75% of the world.

You have or have access to:
1. A computer (most likely with some type of living space to put it in)
2. electricity (that's not as common as you may think)
3. Phone service
4. An ISP connection
5. An e-mail account
6. You live in a country that does not block Internet traffic.
7. You can read.

There is a longer list but you get the point.

When I start on my list of "haves," money isn't at the top.

In material possessions I am enormously wealthy, so are most of you.

We judge assets by how much they are worth.

What you would sell them for indicates their value to you.

How much would you sell your eyes for?

Huh?

How much would you sell your eyes for?

10 million? No.

50 million? No.

1 billion? Probably not.

Your eyes are priceless to you.

Maybe you would let the left eye go for 50 million, but virtually for no amount of money would you part with both of your eyes.

I am enormously wealthy. I have a pair of billion dollar eyes.

You do have something, always know that.

You do have something, be it a billion or a widow's mite.

You do have something.

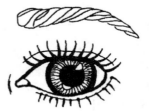

The Bus Driver
============

We were waiting in the blistering sun at the Dollar Car Rental. The shuttle was due in a few minutes to take us to the airport. We were leaving my wife's family reunion in Hartford, CT.

The shuttle was a sight for sore and hot eyes. We had five bags, one a monstrosity of a bag, the king of back-breakers.

The shuttle driver popped out with a wide grin and eagerly began loading the bags onto the bus. "Be careful with that one," I said, pointing to the backbreaker. He was a rather short man, not exactly the Incredible Hulk type.

He tugged and struggled with the bag as it slowly lifted onto the bus. "This kind keeps my voice low," he joked as his voice went into a deep masculine tone as vertebrae creaked under the load.

Before the door closed, the driver went into a one-man comedy act. "Where ya headed?" he inquired. "Atlanta," was the reply.

"Y'all still got possums in Atlanta? The last time I was there many years ago, possums were running across the road by the herd. I was nearly burning the brakes out on my car stopping for all of the possums, then I said what the heck. You ever heard a possum squish under a tire?"

"I hear possum tastes pretty good," was his next remark.

The ride to the airport took about five minutes. It was five minutes of non-stop laughter. He went on and on about this and that with a rather difficult to understand but nevertheless hilarious accent.

He finally said, "You know, I love this job. I get to meet all kinds of people such as y'all nice folks. I can't wait to get up and get to this bus in the morning."

He wasn't talking for a tip, he really loved that bus and his job. It doesn't sound as funny reading it; it was one of those things where you had to be there.
It was a MountainWings Moment.

Here was a job where most would be bored to death. The same five-minute circle over and over all day long. The same bus, the same anxious, hurried, tired, and often rude passengers all day long.

He was in heaven – most would be in hell.

This man had learned one of the great secrets of truly enjoying life. It was in the understanding that joy is not necessarily in the circumstances but in the viewpoint. He saw each passenger load as another opportunity to bring joy into a stranger's world.

They most likely needed it.

If there are angels walking and working among us, maybe they would be doing something like that. . .

. . . and they would be loving it.

The Kingdom of Heaven is truly within.

You know better than to do that!
==========================

1. You have been warned more than once not to do that.

2. You know better than to eat that, it isn't good for you.

3. No, you can't buy that! You have already used up your spare money (if you had any to begin with) on stuff you really didn't need.

4. You need to apologize. The words you spoke in anger hurt.

5. See that fat around your stomach?
   You need to get more exercise.

6. You eat way too many sweets.

7. You watch way too much TV.

8. You are too self-centered; you don't share what you have been blessed with.

9. Yes, it hurts now, but you would not be in this pain if you had done what you knew was right from the start.

10. No matter what it is, a kiss from someone you love will make it better.

These are ten things that I have told my three or six-year-old recently.

What?

Who did you think I was talking to?

Although I have told each of those statements in one form or another to my three or six-year-old, it was in a far gentler form and with great love.

The correction of wrong direction is one of the most difficult portions of parenthood and ministry. Perhaps, that is why adults are so often called "children" in scripture.

Until The Flowers

===============

. . . until the flowers

I am a runner.

I have several circular routes measured from my home.
If I decide to run 3, 4, 5 or 7 miles, each run always ends
at one particular spot.

A few houses down from mine is a home with a beautiful
flower arrangement near the mailbox. The arrangement is
as ornate and as cultured as if a master gardener extended his hand and delicately shaped each flower, bush,
stem, and blade of grass.

I have never seen any flower arrangement as pretty in a
yard.

That's the point.

That's the point that marks the end of my run.

. . . until the flowers.

No matter how long or short the run, I have one goal in mind.

Keep running until I get to the flowers.

Life should be like that.

Keep running until you get to the flowers.

We typically receive the largest number of flowers when our lives are over.

We get the most flowers in our lives at our funeral.

Those flowers don't do you any good.

As far as I know, you can neither see nor smell them.

My neighbors' flowers help give me encouragement and strength to run through this life.

On a recent run, I was thinking about those beautiful bundles of encouragement and had decided to write a MountainWings issue about them. Oddly enough, for the first time, the couple was in the yard working on the flowers as I ended my run.

I ran by their yard; I had almost reached the flowers.
It was a hot sunny day and they could tell by the swelter and sweat that I had been on a grueling run.

The wife spoke, "Could I get you a glass of water or something?" she asked.

"No thanks," I answered.

She didn't realize what they had given me already.

They had given me the flowers.

People who give you flowers for no reason show their giving natures in many ways.

Most people in the neighborhood probably couldn't tell you about my neighbors' flowers. They are probably too busy to see them. They probably see all of the other stuff.

There is much disarray along the run.

There are many weeds and bare branches.
There is trash thrown from cars reflecting people's disregard for others,

. . . and then, there are the flowers.

So it is in life.

Keep your mind on the flowers even when you can't see them.

You can plant flowers.

Not only the physical kind but also flowers of the spirit.

You need to picture the beautiful flowers that await you at the end of your run.

The flowers that never whither or die.

Flowers of the spirit.

You need to understand that they are beautiful and they smell nice.

You also need to tell those who have planted flowers along your path that you appreciate them.

I will print this issue of MountainWings and put it in my neighbors' mailbox.

I doubt that they have ever heard of MountainWings, but their flowers influence MountainWings and in turn, you, on each run.

I am a runner.

So are you.

We run through life, just different paths, different shoes, and different running styles.

In all of your daily running, be sure to stop and smell the roses but

Keep running.

. . . until the flowers.

They Called Me A HERO

======================

I received my blood donor card and on it was written the word "HERO."

I thought all blood donors were called heroes; in reality, anyone who took time to give so freely was a hero in my book.

The Red Cross called my house to ask when would I give blood again. I also figured they did that with all blood donors.

I went to the donation center to donate again, and I asked the nurse, "Do you put 'HERO' on all of the donor cards?"

"No," she replied, "let me see your card."

I pulled the now crumpled card from my wallet and showed it to her. "You have special blood," she commented, "that's why you are called a 'HERO.'"

"Special blood?"

Being a scientist and also being ignorant of the issue, I asked her exactly what did she mean.

She began to explain in detail what I shall greatly condense.

There are two major blood factors: A and B plus the RH factor. If you want to know what the factor and RH are, look them up. It will take too much time to explain properly here.

If you have the A factor, you are type A; the B factor, type B. If you have both factors, you are type AB. If you have the RH factor then you are RH positive.

If you have neither the A nor B factor then you are type O. That's the letter O, not a zero (although it means zero). About one-third of Americans are type O positive. They have neither the A nor B factor but have the RH factor. Type O positives can give blood to a type A positive, type B positive, or type AB positive.

If a person receives blood with a factor that they don't have, the results are usually disastrous, it usually kills them.

The nurse then looked at me and said, "You are type O negative. About 6% of Americans are type O negative. You don't have any factors at all in your blood.

You can give blood to anybody and in many cases, only type O negative blood can be used. Preemie babies can only get type O negative blood. Cancer patients undergoing chemotherapy can only get type O negative blood. Patients with compromised immune systems can only receive type O negative blood. Victims in accidents or other emergency situations can only receive type O negative blood because there is usually no time to do a blood typing test.

Your blood is the hardest of all of the types to keep in stock because so many people need it. That's why you are labeled a hero. Your blood is the universal blood type."

The nurse finished her explanation of why I was called a hero.

That's the short blood type course, now on with the story.

The funny thing is, an O negative can only receive O negative blood. I can only accept blood without factors.

If I ever need blood and receive any blood with factors, it will most likely kill me.

I can give to all, but can only receive from a very select few.

An interesting but appropriate paradox.

I thought about MountainWings as I drove home.

I am a Christian.
I am a Pastor of a Christian church.
I am a heterosexual male.
I am married.

There are other things about me that relate to social, economic, racial, national, educational, and other things that constitute "factors" in life.

I began MountainWings with a dream to be able to lift all. I knew it would reach across a broad spectrum of people. There are subscribers to MountainWings in over 125 countries so:

It spans nationalities.
It spans race.
It spans economic status.
It spans educational achievements.
It spans religious beliefs.
It spans many other factors.

The only factor that it cannot span, is a decision not to be lifted. You cannot lift those who don't want to be lifted.

I realized the full extent of this from a comment from a reader today and that comment prompted me to write this issue.

I publish the comment here minus identifying information.

"I just recently became a subscriber to MountainWings. At first I was going to by-pass it, but I am glad I decided to subscribe.

I am a 64-year-old gay man and must admit, not very religious as I consider myself an Agnostic. However, so many of the MountainWings issues have been so interesting, very moving and yes they do tend to make each day so much more enjoyable.

I eagerly look forward to each new message.

Today's topic took me back to a very fond memory and also gave me much to think about.

Thank you so much for helping to make my life happier."

That was the comment that prompted this issue.

Whether people realize it or not, Jesus had factor-less blood. He associated with those whom society said that he shouldn't. They had factors that weren't acceptable by society and in particular the religious community.

You too can be a hero, but it takes something special to reach out to someone who may have different factors than yourself.

All of us are born with factors of one type or another.

If you are born the child of happy multimillionaire parents, you have a different set of factors than if you are born the child of drug addicts. Those factors will affect you.

When you have many resources, you have the ability to help many. When you have few resources and a lot of factors, you can only help a few. The real hero is not based on the resources.

It's not based on the blood. It's based on the willingness to give of whatever you have.

Most with O negative don't give of what they have.

They are those with a great ability to help a lot of people. Most don't.

The thing is, neither do most with AB positive. AB positives can only help a select few. Most struggle themselves and the last thing on their minds is helping others.

Take this bit of advice.
When you help another, it lifts the burden from you.
I can't psychologically explain it, but I know it happens.
In helping others you forget about your own situation
and you realize that you are not in such bad shape after all.

It's really not so much a matter of what flows in you,
it's only what flows out that will make a difference in the world.

You are a hero just waiting to come forth;
there is no better time to begin than now.

Feel it pulsing within your veins now with the thump-thump of each heartbeat.

He-ro, He-ro, He-ro

When you realize what you really are and the potential within, you won't be able to resist being a hero.

It's in your blood.

GO REST

=========

Stop – Do NOTHING!!!

You need to rest and take a break sometimes.

I can go into a long psychological and physiological explanation of why you need to do this but most of you instinctively know this.

You know that you need to stop, rest, and take a break sometimes.

We all know it but often we are slaves, and slaves aren't usually given sufficient rest.

Most of you are saying, "I'm not a slave!"

This is the EXACT dictionary definition of a slave:
slave n. 1. One bound in servitude as the property of a person or household. 2. One who is abjectly subservient to a specified person or influence. 3. One who works extremely hard.

According to statistics, we now work longer than ever.

Two jobs, or one job that we work more than 50 hours a week is commonplace.

Why? Because we often feel that we have to.

Money is not usually stacked in the bank. We are usually slaving to pay current bills.

I was on the board of directors of a bank for years.
The determining factor in how much to lend someone is not how much they can comfortably pay, but how much they can pay under a strain.

When looking for a house, most don't consider how much they can comfortably pay, but how much the bank will lend them.

The number one credit card world wide is called, MASTERcard.

The name is no accident.

If one is the Master, that means the other is the . . .
The CARD is usually the master.

Yes, and the best slave is the one who doesn't realize it.

The high credit card bills, the high mortgages and rent, the high car notes, etc. make it where most can't even take some relaxing time for themselves.

We have become slaves and don't realize it.
Divine law tries to prevent us from becoming slaves.

We are all familiar with the Ten Commandments whether we agree with them or not. The first commandment where we are told something to do is the fourth commandment. It says to work six days and to rest on the seventh day.

That's a principle not only of human flesh, it's a principle of dirt. Any good farmer will tell you that to get maximum production from farm land, you need to plant six years and let the ground sit idle for the seventh year.

I own my business.

That can enslave you more than working for someone else, if you let it.

The key is to recognize truth.

Recognize an enslaver, whether it is a job, a business, a car, a relationship, or whatever wraps you so tightly that you can't even rest once a week or once in a while.

You don't have to go to Jamaica. Go spend a weekend with Grandma. Go somewhere and do exactly what I am about to tell you.

Go rest, you deserve it, and you shouldn't be a slave.

The outline of your duties while you rest is between the quotes:

"   "

The Weather

===========

I never really know what the weather will be.

I belong to five of the most weather conscious groups around.

I jog, I ride a motorcycle, I have a boat, I am a pilot, and I live, eat and breathe.

All of the above can be severely influenced, both good and bad, by the weather.

Today is a particularly beautiful day.

When the sun is shining on a cloudless day, the visibility is unlimited. The warm sun is perfect for virtually any outdoor activity. It's nice; the old, middle aged, and young enjoy it.

The plants grow fast and strong on such days.

When it is raining, you can sleep better. There is nothing more soothing than water cascading down in the constant pitter-patter of nature's rhythm.

Even jogging in the rain is refreshing.

I never forget that without rain I would starve. There would eventually be no water to make the crops grow, drought would abound, and millions would die.

Storms charge the air with an almost mystical feeling. The elders would say amidst the thunder and lightening, "Be still, God is moving!"

Freezing temperatures help to kill flies, mosquitoes, and fleas. If you have pets, you know the flea season is really rough after a mild winter.

Sun, rain, storms, heat, and freezing temperatures all have their place in the cycles of nature. They all are beautiful.

So it is with our lives. We have our seasons and our weather.

Sun, rain, storms, heat, and freezing temperatures all have their place in the cycles of our lives.

We have things to grow, dreams to water, pests to kill, and moments to simply stand in awe and watch God move.

The seasons of our lives.

Do you belong to one of the most weather conscious groups around?

What's the weather like today?

It's great for living, eating, and breathing.

Yes...
It's a beautiful day.

Back Around Up
===============

A famous quote says, "sorry looks back, worry looks around, faith looks up."

There is absolutely nothing that you can do about yesterday, last year, or the last century.

There are a multitude of things that I would have done differently if I could do them over.
Maybe I would be in better shape but who knows?

I wouldn't have fallen off my motorcycle at 14 if I could do it over. That hurt.

But if I hadn't fallen off, I wouldn't have become such a seat belt advocate. Many of my family members had major auto crashes and may have been killed if they hadn't been wearing their seat belts. They might not have had them on if I hadn't fallen off of that motorcycle.

But that hurt.

There are so many things that we would do differently if we could because we would eliminate the hurt.

BUT YOU CAN'T - SO GET OVER IT!!!

How many of you are doing fine "under the circumstances?"

UNDER? That's right, UNDER.

"Circum" means around, "stance" means where you stand
or your point of view.

So whatever is "around" your "attitude and point of view"
are your circumstances.

Many times, you can't change what's around you,
but you can change your attitude and point of view.

When you change that for the better, you'll get out from
UNDER your circumstances.

Stop worrying.

There isn't a thing that worrying will help.
There is plenty that worrying will hurt.
If it can't help anything but can hurt plenty,
is it wise to worry?

Of course not.

Faith believes that things will get better.
Wisdom sees that it's pretty good now.
Thankfulness knows that it could be a lot worse.

You are NOT Under Your Circumstances!

Unless of course, that's where you stand on the issue.

The Big Lottery Winner
==================

How would you feel if you won the lottery?

I mean a really big one, like 100 million or so?

Pretty good huh?

That's what I thought.

If you won 100 million dollars, that would undoubtedly make your day. It won't make your life but I will admit, it will do a pretty good job of making your day.

It would be hard to convince anyone that you weren't very fortunate if you won a big lottery.

Which prize is greater, money or life?

Do you know how many sperm are released from the average male during the act of procreation?

Approximately 300 million sperm are released. Only one fertilizes the egg.

Each sperm will produce a different person with different characteristics.

300 million sperm compete in a race to fertilize the egg.

The one that wins makes the baby.

You won.

Out of 300 million, you won.

You got life.

The lottery has odds of around fifty something million to one.

You won a race with odds of 300 million to one.

You won a greater prize than money in a race with greater odds than the lottery.

You won life.

Studies have shown that most big lottery winners aren't as happy five years later. I have a friend who knew two people who won over 50 million dollar lotteries. I asked my friend, "were your friends happier before they won or now?"

My friend paused in deep thought as he compared in his mind his friends before and after their big winnings. "They were happier before they won," my friend replied.

I know countless who have won the prize of life.

Unfortunately, some, like the big lottery winners, often end up sad.

The thing about life. . .

Not only did you win the initial race, each morning that you wake up, you've won again.

Don't be like the typical big lottery winner.

Celebrate the win. Celebrate the day.

Recognize the prize. Each day.

CLOSET SPACE

==============

Is your closet too crowded?

Perhaps the single greatest indicator of the overload that we have in life are closets.

They are packed.

It doesn't matter how big our closets are.

Sooner or later we fill them up.

Why?

There is a closet rule of life that states:

1. Clothes expand to fill all available closet space
2. Sooner or later if you keep getting more clothes,
   you either have to:
      A. Get more closet space
      B. Get rid of some clothes

2 B is what we hate to do.

But if we are TO BE what we are TO BE, we need to learn the rule of 2B and get rid of some clothes.

Time is like closet space. We have a limited amount of it.

We keep putting more and more things in until our time is cluttered.

The more cluttered it gets, the more things are out of place.

The time that we should be sleeping, we've got something else in that space.

The time that we should be spending with family, we've got something else in that space.

The time that we should have to ourselves to do whatever we do to help our spirit, we've got something else in that space.

Even as our closet hinges strain to keep from bursting, we still try to put more stuff in.

Take a look around your closet of time right now.

How much has accumulated that you should have gotten rid of long ago?

They still may be good clothes, but your closet is just too full.

We have habits that we formed in our teenage years that should have long ago been removed from our closets.

Some even have friends who should have long ago been removed, for they no longer fit our style or destination.

As you change and grow, you should change what's in your closet.

Maybe we don't need more stuff in the closet.

Maybe we don't need a bigger closet.

Maybe we just need to clean out some stuff and not with the purpose to make room for more stuff.

We may just need some space,

in a lot of areas,

for a lot of reasons.

There is a spiritual saying that tells you to go into your closet to pray.

For many of us, there's simply no room.

Go look at your bedroom closet right now.

Chances are, it will reflect your closet of time.

Eyes From Above

==============

I walked into the store as I had done countless times before.

There was nothing unusual about the night, just a routine stroll down the aisles of commerce. My five and two-year-old sons were with me.

It was a huge store. You would know the name of the chain, but the name doesn't matter.

Bright lights, wide aisles, and full shelves made for an awesome store. My sons naturally were interested in the toy section, so there we strolled.

The modern stores don't have many helpers like the old days.

I used to work in a drug store. My job was to price merchandise, stock the shelves, sweep the floor, ring the cash register, and watch customers.

I didn't watch customers for fun. Customers would steal in the old days. My job included helping customers find what they wanted but keeping a watchful eye to make sure they paid for what they found.

Those old days came to mind as I wandered or rather was towed by anxious kids down the huge aisles.

How in the world do they keep people from stealing

them blind?

There were no clerks or assistants watching us. What was to prevent us from pocketing any number of tempting items?

I looked around, not for the purpose of stealing anything, but of scientific curiosity.

How did they keep people from stealing?

I knew the nature of people had not improved since I was a clerk. People stole then and they steal now.

This was an extremely successful chain. Surely they couldn't be this trusting. Surely they couldn't be this benevolent that they would simply allow people to have whatever they felt like not paying for.

Surely not.

I am a scientist. I think. I analyze. I wonder. I seek answers. I am a businessman. No people watching, plenty of merchandise, a certain percentage of people who would take advantage of inattention, successful chain stores, it didn't fit. How could they trust so?

They didn't. That much I knew. I know the commercial mind.

They couldn't and didn't trust people that much.

So why was no one watching?

I knew that couldn't be either.

Maybe they were watching.

If so, then how were they watching?

I knew if they were watching it would have to be through video cameras. I knew where they would need to be positioned.

I looked up.

Whoa!

As many times as I had been in that store and similar stores of the chain, I had never thought to look up. I walked beneath totally unaware and unconcerned about the eyes above.

As I looked up, I saw rows and rows of surveillance cameras.

Somewhere between 100 and 200 cameras looked down as I surveyed the roof of the huge store.

If you didn't know already, you wouldn't know they were cameras but I knew. Surveillance cameras are usually mounted behind blue colored domes. You can't see in, but the camera can see out. It can point in any direction, and you don't know if and where it is looking.

It can swivel, tilt, pan, and zoom. They can follow your every move. They can zoom out to view the whole aisle or zoom in on a pimple. Hundreds of them and I never

knew or guessed because I never thought about it.
It was a MountainWings Moment.

Eyes from above that watched every move of those
below.

So many walk without realizing every move is observed
and recorded.

Eyes from above.

I walked differently once I saw the cameras. I had no
intention of ever doing anything wrong, with or without
cameras; I just walked differently knowing that someone
could be watching every single move that I made.

It shouldn't have made a difference.

But it did.

We often go through life as if no one sees.

As if no eyes from above are watching.

Suppose we realized that?

Every frown, every harsh word, every wrong deed, every
good or bad twitch of our minds and muscles...

Recorded.

Eyes from above.

Encased in a blue canopy.

It makes you walk differently once you realize that.

It really does.

Glide
=====

Jogging is a world of experience by itself.

After 3 miles or so, I felt a pain in my left leg.

Not a major pain, it just felt like the beginning of a cramp.

I began to limp. I didn't want to put any excess pressure on the leg because I had over three miles to go even if I turned around and headed straight back, and I wasn't at the halfway point yet.

Something said, "Glide."

Glide?

I began to notice how I was running with the limping action.

My gait was uneven. It was awkward. I didn't know the exact kinetics, but I knew the un-rhythmic motion was putting additional strain on my leg muscles.

So I began to glide.

I focused on running smoothly.
I let my feet touch the pavement as light as possible.
Like a swan skimming over a lake, I concentrated to make each step as graceful as possible.

Within a minute, my left leg felt fine.

It was a MountainWings Moment.

Often when pain hits us, we lose our grace and become awkward.

We shuffle, stumble, bumble, weave, wobble, hobble, and stagger.

If we just glide and stay smooth, often the pain goes away because the rough motion makes it worse, not better.

Someone criticizes us. . . OUCH!
We shuffle, stumble, bumble, weave, wobble, hobble, and stagger.

Someone offends us. . . OUCH!
We shuffle, stumble, bumble, weave, wobble, hobble, and stagger.

Someone has a difference of opinion. . . OUCH!
We shuffle, stumble, bumble, weave, wobble, hobble, and stagger.

Someone doesn't respond the way we think they should
. . . OUCH!
We shuffle, stumble, bumble, weave, wobble, hobble, and stagger.

Instead of maintaining our peace, the smooth gait, we become frustrated. That makes the pain worse, not better.

Instead of forgiving and forgetting, we retaliate and remember.

That often makes the pain worse.

Many of life's pains would go away if we'd just learn to glide.

Yes, it hurts, but the shuffling and stumbling usually doesn't help.

While jogging (or with any exercise), if pain starts, it's usually wise to just stop. This was more a spiritual revelation, yet it applied to physical things.

If we can keep our movements, thoughts, emotions, and spirit smooth, that often takes us right over the rough things.

Glide

I wan to sey mi preyers agin
=======================

On the nights that I put the two oldest boys to bed, the 6 and 3-year-old, we hold hands and pray.

Only the 6-year-old and I pray. The 3-year-old (Josees) usually remains quiet.

Tonight, I asked Josees to simply say "Thank You Jesus." I figured I would try to get him to say something in prayer.

In his still garbled and yet undeveloped speech, he said as best he could, "Than chu Jesus."

I then prayed.

Usually, after I pray, we all hug and exchange goodnight kisses.

Josees always leaves a cold wet spot on my forehead, but it is a spot that soothes and washes away any trials of the day.

This time as I said "Amen," Josees said, "Daddy, I wan to sey mi preyers agin."

"Ok," I mumbled, somewhat startled.

Josees in his garbled speech prayed one of the most touching prayers that I have ever heard. He thanked God for his family individually by name, for his bike (actually a tricycle), his bed, the house, and a host of other things.

It was a MountainWings Moment.

The kids had taught me something about praying. They focused on the immediate things. The many things they could see.

El, the 6-year-old, thanks God for his pillow, the dresser drawers, the dresser, the mirror, his bed spread, his bed, his socks, his shoes, and a host of other things that I never thought about.

Is it the early stages of materialism?

No, it is the early stages of being appreciative for the things most take for granted.

When I first heard El pray, I had to ask myself, "Had I ever thanked God for my drawers and my pillow?"
I didn't think so.

I use them every day but had never given thanks for them.

Children teach us a lot.
I have never heard El ask for anything while praying.
He only thanks God for what he has been given.
He has his wants, believe me, but in prayer, he only gives thanks.

Often after listening to the sincere prayers of a child, I realize how much I have never thanked God for.

I have had to bow before I went to bed and ask in my heart,

"Father, can I say my prayers again."

"And a little child shall lead them."

Extraction
`=========`

My young son had his two front teeth removed today.

It's amazing how much the lives of children parallel the lives of adults.

Many of the same things they go through, adults go through.

The statement, "The only difference between men and boys is the price of their toys" makes sense when you analyze the behavior of men and boys.

My son had to go through an extraction.

His two front teeth had cavities. They had begun to hurt.

Something had to be done to ease the pain.

I talked with the dentist and he gave me two choices, fix them or remove them.

I asked, "what's the advantages and disadvantages of each?"

"If you repair the tooth and cap them, there is a 32% chance the tooth will become infected and you will have to remove it, if you remove it, that ends it." the dentist said.

"Which is more traumatic on the child?" I asked.

"It's about the same either way," the dentist said.

Many times in life we have the same decision.

There is something rotten in our world.

We can try to fix it. That may work or it may not.

Sometimes the rotten things that we try to fix end up becoming even more rotten, and we have to remove them anyway.

We can decide to just remove them from the start and minimize the future potential problems.

Everyone has some rotten teeth in their lives. We instantly know which ones they are. By rotten teeth, I don't necessarily mean teeth but things that are attached to us that have decayed and in one form or another are causing us pain.

Those are rotten teeth.

Even when speaking about teeth, you know exactly how many bad teeth you have, don't you?

Answer the question, how many bad teeth do you have?

This next question about your teeth shows you the difference between a mountain climber and one who smacks into the mountain.

How many good teeth do you have?

Huh?

I asked, "How many good teeth do you have?"
You don't know do you?

That's because the world teaches us to focus on the bad.

If you don't believe me, look at the evening news today.
Count the number of minutes devoted to bad news
versus the number of minutes devoted to good news.
You will see what I mean.

That's why you don't know how many good teeth you have.

You know you are supposed to have 32 teeth, but you
have never counted them for sure.

Maybe you've got a few extra teeth.
You don't know if you haven't counted them.

Stop right now and count your good teeth. . .

I'll continue the lesson on extraction tomorrow, but I want
you to learn to consciously recognize the good things in
your life first, then I'll tell you the lesson of the
extraction.

By the way. I have exactly 32 good teeth. Some are very
crooked, but they work and they don't hurt. Some have
had dental work, but they work and they don't hurt.
Four have had root canals, but they work and they don't
hurt. They are good teeth, but they aren't perfect.

Count your good stuff today before the news comes on.

COUNT THEM! BEFORE THE NEWS COMES ON

Extraction #2
= = = = = = = = = = =

Yesterday I asked you to count how many good teeth you have.

So you now know how many good teeth you have.

Did you notice something?

For the vast majority, the number of good teeth FAR outnumbers the bad.

You have far more good teeth, but it's the bad teeth that get all of the attention. One bad tooth can cause us so much pain that we forget about all of the good.

So it is with life.

One bad relationship and we think all men/women are bad.

One bad experience with a member of a different race, religion or culture and we think all who are different from us are bad.

A company can have a thousand employees and we can have one bad experience with an obnoxious employee and we think the whole company is bad.

One bad apple doesn't spoil the whole bunch, but it will eventually spoil the whole bunch if you don't remove the bad apple. Infection spreads.

Some things you have to extract to keep them from spoiling the whole bunch.

My son had to get his two front teeth extracted to prevent further pain and to even prevent the spread of infection to the rest of his body.

Extraction of things in our lives is often necessary but seldom pleasant.

He had to be sedated, strapped down, and numbed.
He still hollered.

Eagles fly high, but have you ever noticed eagles don't have a lot of stuff strapped on their backs?

Some of us haven't reached the heights that we are destined to reach because we haven't extracted some things. It's too much on our backs and in our spirits.

You know what things they are.

As plain as I am writing this and as clear as you can see these letters, you know what things in your life need extracting.

We all have them.

Extraction hurts but the continuing pain of decay hurts even worse and for much longer.

I counsel quite a few people.

More often than not, they will have major problems by the time they schedule counseling. As I listen to their situation, I can often see things or a different perspective on the thing that they cannot. Many are helped through counseling.

Even though I can often see things that they cannot, most of the stuff that they need to change, THEY ALREADY KNOW!

"I know I need to do this"
"I know I need to change that"
"I know this is wrong"
"I know I shouldn't feel this way"
"I know I should leave this relationship"
"I know this is not good"

"I know I should. . . "

Many already know the things in their life that need to be extracted.

So do you.

The problem is not the knowledge in many instances.
It's the pain of extraction.

Pulling anything with deep roots is a problem.

The closer anyone is to a child and the further they are from maturity, the more sedation, straps and numbing they will need.

A child will even endure the paid for months or years until the tooth eventually falls out from the decay.

Often we endure the pain far longer than necessary until it falls out and has nearly knocked us out.

Learn the lesson of extraction.

For though we may have far more good teeth, this is a lesson we all need to know.

MountainWings.com is about helping to lift you over the mountains of life.

Sometimes what you need is not really a lift.
You just need to remove some things.

Just as a hot air balloon is mired to the ground with sand-bags, often so are we.

It's not that we don't have the wind to fly, we've just got too many sandbags.

Some need to be extracted and then we can fly.

Mama Has Long School
====================

. . .and a little child shall lead you.

Children can teach us many things.

My son, the 5-year-old one, taught me another lesson.

He goes to school at 8:30 each morning.

He is typical of virtually all children and prefers to stay at home. He has his usual whining about school each morning. My wife will either pick him up at 1 p.m. or 3 p.m. depending on her schedule.

She started taking classes twice each week to get her real estate broker's license. Her classes are from 9 a.m. to 5 p.m. It is a 1 hour drive in the rush hour traffic to get to the class. That means she is out of the house by 8 a.m. twice each week and doesn't get home until after 6 p.m.

On those days, I take my son to school.

This was one of those days.

He was unusually quiet and cooperative.

As we pulled into the school parking lot he said,
"You know daddy, mama has to go to school a lot longer
than I do."

I hadn't thought of it in those terms; neither had he until
this morning.

He learned the important lesson of relativity.

All things in the material world are relative.

His school didn't seem so bad now. Mama was gone
from early until late. He was only at school until early
afternoon. Suddenly things weren't so bad.

Life is relative.

Complaining about the job that you have to go to early
each day?

Think about the over 10,000 I.T. workers laid off last
month.

Complaining about the husband who won't help wash the
dishes or the wife who uses paper plates instead of wash-
ing dishes?

Think about the ones who took off and never came home
for dinner.

Complaining about the extra bit of fat around your
stomach?

Think about all those whose ribs show from lack of food.

"You know daddy, mama has to go to school a lot longer than I do."

Mama, exhausted from class all day, housework, childcare and driving, looks at her son and says, "boy, he sure has it easy."

Others look at mama and say, "boy, she sure has it easy, only two kids and a good husband."

Life is relative. Learn to see your blessings.

Though you, like my son, carry a heavy load based on your perception,

Boy, you sure have it easy.

At Times Like These
= = = = = = = = = = = = = = = = = =

"Please pray the prayer of intercession for my husband and me. We are going through difficulties regarding 'his duties' and 'my duties.' I am at home caring for our two small children and my invalid mother. At times, the house is not up to par. I realize that I don't do all that I can. It's at these times when I need his understanding the most.
Please pray for us...........
Thank you"

This is a prayer request sent to MountainWings. It is used with permission and shall remain anonymous. When I read it to pray over the request, it struck me. I could feel the anguish, but I could also feel myself.

We react most to things that we can relate to; to things that we have gone through or are going through.

I don't stay at home with the kids, my mother actually helps us.

My wife, the children and I are doing great.

So what part struck me?

"It's at these times when I need his understanding the most."

All of us have "at times like these..." moments. There are times when we have not done all that we could and even times when we have done all that we could, but it just doesn't seem to be enough.

It is at times like those when we are at our weakest. Any honest person will tell you that they have them too. They are unavoidable because we are human and life has stuff.

Maybe you will read a MountainWings issue and it is just "off."

Maybe I wrote it in "one of those times."

People often expect perfection from pastors. We can't be perfect because the world isn't perfect and neither are we. We all have "times like those."

All of us have times like those. Remember that.

Remember that every person you meet, in every place that you go, will have times like those. You have no way of knowing whether they are going through one of those times right now.

You will need understanding when you go through.

So will they.

Remember that.

The First and The Last Mile
=====================

I just finished jogging. It's 7:12 a.m.

During the run, many revelations came that paralleled this morning's run to life.

There are two very difficult miles to run no matter how long the run.

The First and the Last Mile.

I usually run five miles or more.

The first mile is the hardest and the one most missed. You see, you have to get started to run the first mile.

It's hard to get started.

I have to get out of bed.

Those first few steps that wake a sleeping body are part of the first mile.

They are tougher than the steepest hill.

You have a race to run, a course to complete, or a project that awaits you.

You too have a first mile. And your first mile is tough, just like mine.

When I take my first step outside, most of my run is completed.

I've accomplished the hardest part.
I've gotten started and stepped out.

The next few steps bring out the stiffness of your body as the muscles stretch and your lungs fill with the crisp, cool morning air. It's still dark outside and menacing shadows reach out from strange corners.

Darkness creates a different, somewhat eerie world.
There could be dangers in the shadows but danger usually doesn't get up this early.

If there are any aches and pains, the first mile will bring them out.

The greatest probability that you will give up and turn back is in the first mile.

The vast majority make new year's resolutions each year.
Most have broken them at the end of the first two weeks.
The first two weeks are the first mile.

Miles 2, 3 and 4 are usually uneventful, but the last mile is a doozy.

There is something about the last mile that's a real strain, and it doesn't matter whether I am running 2 miles or 10 miles. The last mile is a real strain.

And so it is with life.

To get started is a strain.

To finish is a strain.

The First and The Last Mile

What's your first mile?

Half A Sugar
===========

I handle a lot in the business world.

I manage two companies and pastor a church. I make
decisions, put out fires, deal with people, handle disputes
among employees and customers, handle the finances
when things are tight, and all of the other myriad of
things that go along with running anything.

Plus, I write most of the original MountainWings issues.

All of that plus a little more equals about half a sugar.

What's a sugar?

That's my two-year-old son.

I call him "The Sugar," but his name is Josees.

He is the sweetest little boy in the world, but The Sugar
is busy.

I kept The Sugar and my oldest son (he's five) tonight
while my wife went to a meeting.

When The Sugar and the five-year-old get together,
it puts The Sugar in turbo mode.

Men, if you don't know what turbo mode is, just ask any
mother of a child two or older.

With adults under my supervision and payroll, I have some authority. They listen quite attentively if I ever raise my voice. Although material power is lacking in many respects, it does have mankind's respect.

Not so with The Sugar. The Sugar doesn't give a hoot.

The Sugar represents many of the things in life.
Many of the things in life don't give a hoot about power, authority, education, money, or how eloquent you speak.

There is nothing that I have that's more precious than my two boys. Yet, there is not much in an ordinary day that will top a few hours with the two little darlings in exasperation.

Life often gives us our greatest loves and greatest challenges all rolled up into one person or thing.

When my wife got home she said:
"How did that food get on The Sugar's head?"
"How did that spot get on the sofa?"
"Why is his shirt wet?"
"How did all of this stuff get in the middle of the floor?"

That was just the first 30 seconds after she got home.
She couldn't fathom how I let things get so out of hand.

The answer to those questions. . .

That's another issue. . . a long one.

Boy, was I glad to hear the garage door go up signaling the arrival of my wife.

I pretended like it was a breeze handling the two darlings.

It was.

It was just a 100 miles per hour breeze.

I saw a bumper sticker on a van with child seats. It read: "Get a real job, be a housewife."

The Sugar has made me appreciate that bumper sticker.

Two businesses, a church, MountainWings

Half a sugar

About the same

UP Beat or Beat Up?
==================

My husband, Edward has always been one to give the shirt off his back, literally, or to give his last bit of change.

He never asks for anything in return, and he is a very hard worker and provides well for his family. Recently, I had knee surgery and gall bladder surgery, and he worked and took care of me and still had time for our three kids, all less than 11 years of age.

It just seems that nothing ever goes his way and now we have been kicked out of our home of six years so our landlord can move her friends in. We have to find another place to live soon ...and I know we will.

I just feel so bad that no matter how hard Edward tries, he never gets anything or anywhere. I spend a lot of time trying to understand how someone like him stays so upbeat.

I have prayed for guidance, and I have prayed for silly things like for him to be chosen for something of value. I realize we are blessed with three happy, healthy children and fairly good health ourselves, but now my prayers are just that he may receive a pat on the back or something just to give him a little boost to go on trudging through what seems to be a meager existence here in the Ozarks in Missouri.

Just let him know he is worth more than any house or

any amount of money we could ever have.
We all love him!!!

Thanks for your time and thanks for your prayers.
Verna Torres

From MountainWings.com:

You said, "I spend a lot of time trying to understand how someone like him stays so upbeat."

It looks like your husband has found one of the keys to inner peace. He is healthy, he has a job, he has healthy children, and he has a wife and children who love him and wish that he had more.

I understand why he is so upbeat.

That is the difference of perspective. Proper outlook on your blessings will make you feel upbeat. Focusing on the things that you don't have will make you feel beat up.

It all depends on which way you look at it.
UP Beat or BEAT Up.

Edward realizes that he has been chosen for something of great value and that he has something of great value.

"The father of godly children has cause for joy.
What a pleasure it is to have wise children."
Proverbs 23:24

A salute to Edward Torres, Lebanon, MO USA

You Won't Get Your Money Back

==============================

"You won't get your money back," she said.

If I had to paint a picture of stately elegance, it would have been as if she jumped from the canvas of my mind into real life.

She was the teacher.

You won't get your money back.

The words pierced me as though she was talking to me. She wasn't.
She was talking to another student.
It was like one of those high powered bullets that can go through several people and a car without even slowing down.

You won't get your money back, kept echoing off the walls of my head like a BB in an empty corn flakes box.

To most of the students in the class it was just a statement.

It was more than that to me.

I saw a whole attitude of life in that simple statement. Maybe it was her. Often it's not what you say, but who says it.

She was the teacher.

She spoke softly, yet underneath you could feel she had a depth of knowledge and wisdom that didn't come from her Yale degree. It was polished by Yale, but didn't originate there.

You won't get your money back.

A student had asked the teacher, "What if I don't produce anything in this class? What if I freeze up? What if I come away from this series of workshops and have nothing? What if I draw a blank?"

They were honest questions.
The class was about creativity and that's something that no one can force. It was possible that you could draw a blank. What if you did?

The teacher said, "If you do draw that blank, you won't get your money back."

I always choose my teachers carefully, for you become a part of what they are. I felt very comfortable with this choice. She reminded me so much of life. She was full. She was a grandmotherly type with sparkling hair like spun silk. She was someone's grandmother I was sure.

Though she had a degree from Yale, she spoke with wisdom more like a grandmother than a college professor

I could hear the grandmotherly wisdom dodge and duck its way around the fine parchment of the Yale degree and silently shout to ears that hear more than sound, "If you miss out on what you've paid for, life won't give you your money back."

We've all paid for the class of life. The minute the doctor eased our heads out of our mother's womb, we got a full scholarship.

Your joy is all paid for. Your adventure is all paid for. Your tingles, thrills, and exciting moments of discovering every wonder imaginable are all paid for.

We are all students in the class of life.
Some of us will get more out of it than others.
Some will nod off and miss most of what life has to offer.
Some will cut class and leave early, never to return.
Some will get distracted and miss the main points.
Others will soak it in, learn, grow, and glow.

There are those who will get more than their money's worth, every minute in every class in an ever-unfolding adventure.

Another group spend their time watching a clock that freezes motionless like a shy freckled-faced girl when eyes fall upon her and stare.

You are in class, get all that you can.

If you miss out, you won't get your money back.

The Place

=========

I took my two oldest boys somewhere recently that they enjoyed so much they didn't want to come back home.

It was a place where there were all kinds of rides and fun things to see, do and play with. Every town has one of these places no matter how small.

I know people are on a tight budget nowadays, but I truly believe this is a place everyone can afford if they really wanted to.

I can remember my parents carrying me to this place many times and how much fun I had as a little boy, and I'm sure you do to.

Even though it seems like you could stay there all day and night, they do have a closing time and then you have to go home.

The place I am talking about is outside.

No I'm not talking about a town fair or carnival that is outside. I am simply talking about just plain old outside.

The rides I was referring to are tricycles and bicycles.

The fun things to see, do and play with are flowers, dirt, sticks, and pine cones. The closing time is when the lights turn down (the Sun). The memories are priceless but the cost is also priceless.

That's right, it is free to go outside.

I took my kids outside the other day and what a time they had.

The older we get in life the more it takes to entertain and fascinate us. Most adults would not get the same thrill out of an amusement park as kids get out of going outside.

Many times what we think our kids want and need are not what they actually want and need. A child would grow tired of playing with a $1,000 remote controlled helicopter by themselves faster than they would just blowing dandelions into the wind and watching it's miniature parachutes land.

You see with kids, it's not just what they have or do more so than it is with whom.

Children value time and attention from parents much more than gifts. I bought my young boys their own set of drums each. Sure they played with them a lot the first week, but after that they have more fun if I get down on the kitchen floor with them, turn over three pots and beat on them with spoons and spatulas.

Don't mistake me, I never said Mom enjoyed hearing the "noise" nor does she enjoy the thought of beating on her good pots and pans. But it warms her heart just to know her kids have a tight bond with their father.

I bought my kids the best brand new $300 video game with extra controls, the latest games and even got extra

memory to save the place in the game. A week later,
I packed it all up and took it back to the store. I had just
spent over $500 on a game that had the latest 3D graphics.
I was frustrated on one hand but learned a valuable
lesson on the other.

I took them outside and got some pine cones and handed
them a stick; I was the pitcher and they were the batters.
No game on the expensive console could match the
laughter and enjoyment that my kids showed while
knocking a home run (hitting the pine cone out of the yard)
with a stick.

The next time you want to give your kids the very best in
entertainment try a neat place called outside.

A MountainWings Original by James Bronner

The Big Flash
===========

For those of you who are old enough to remember, what you were doing when you heard the news that President Kennedy had been shot?

I was almost 7 years old.

I was walking down a large hill leading to our house on Rockmart Drive heading home from school. Someone pulled up beside me in a car and said, "President Kennedy has been shot."

That's been almost 40 years ago and though I was just a small boy, the memory vividly lingers.

Major traumatic events freeze the moment like a camera's flash. It is a picture that remains and even time itself doesn't erase it.

Most Americans remember what they were doing when a traumatic event occurred.

February 6 is such a day for me.

The day has no special meaning for most of you, but for me it's one of those flash days. It's not exactly the typical Kodak moment.

It is the day my brother died.
I remember receiving a 911 page on my beeper. I had been in the shower and didn't answer the phone.

When I returned the call, it was my youngest brother telling me that my 38-year-old brother had been taken to the hospital after passing out.

It was Sunday morning. I was due to deliver the Sunday morning message in church in two hours. I rushed to the hospital. Only my brother's wife was there when I arrived. She explained the events of the morning.

Although I knew from the description it sounded medically serious, I knew my brother was a young, healthy, and vibrant man.

The thought of death seemed impossible.

Two of his neighbors were doctors and they rode in the ambulance with him and even went into the emergency room to assist.

When his neighbor walked out of the emergency room and walked past us shaking his head, he spoke no words. The gesture and look was enough to convey the meaning.

This couldn't be. . . and yet it was.

It was the greatest mountain that I had ever faced.

It was a blinding flash.

He had a blood clot in his leg that migrated to his lungs.

He had complained of difficulty breathing and had gone to the hospital several days earlier. The doctors ran tests and said that he was fine and sent him home.

If he had been diagnosed properly, anti-clotting drugs could have easily dissolved the clot before it did fatal damage.

Often mountains are caused by the failure of others to do their job properly.

People will make mistakes. You will make mistakes. I will make mistakes.

Of all of the sermons that I have preached, I can only remember the exact date and subject of one, the sermon that I preached on that Sunday morning.

There was nothing fantastic about the sermon just as there was nothing fantastic about my downhill walk on the day President Kennedy was shot.

But it was a sermon preached in the light of a flash. You remember everything in the light of a flash.

In my mind I was tempted to change my prepared sermon and deliver a message appropriate to the moment. A still small voice said, "no, deliver that which you have been given."

The message was entitled, "Would Jesus be happy with your giving?"

I later understood the importance of that message in light of the events of that day. When we leave this world, it won't be important what we've gotten, but rather what we gave. All of our accumulations and possessions won't really matter.

Great mountains will change you. They are the challenges and the obstacles that will either make you stronger or break you.

They will make you better or bitter;
a climber or a complainer.

The mountain will allow you to see a vision that you can't see from the valley.

The mountain can also make you cringe so with the fear of falling that you tightly clamp your eyes shut.

You can revel in the pure rarefied air.

You can gasp for breath from the thinness of it.

The mountain can do great or terrible things.

It depends on both perspective and preparation.

A flash can change your life like none other.

It can either blind you or illuminate dark areas where you could not see. It depends on both perspective and preparation. The Kennedy flash I remember very well, but it didn't change me.

I was never the same after the February 6 flash.
I later preached a sermon about how the experience changed my life.

It is still one of the most downloaded and listened to sermons on AirJesus.com.

It's called "1 Hour and 40 Minutes."

If you ever have a flash of the loss of a loved one, go and listen to that message.

It will help you fly over that mountain.

I shouldn't say "if" you ever have a flash of the loss of a loved one.

If you live long enough, you will have several.

Those types of flashes MUST come. It is an inevitable part of life. You cannot stop them and often can't even delay them.

The flashes are not the problem. The problem is not being prepared to fly when the inevitable flashes come.

How do you prepare for a flash?
You don't.

You learn to live each day to the best of your ability and to see the beauty.

You learn to laugh at the traffic jam instead of cursing it.
You learn to smile when someone attacks you.
You learn to have patience when the grocery checkout line stands still.

You learn to handle the little things.

The little things prepare you for the big flashes.

When my brother left this earth, I could honestly say that I had done everything as an older brother that I could have done for him in life.

When he went to the hospital days earlier, I laid my hands on him and prayed a prayer of comfort and peace.

He told his wife later that he felt a warm glow go over him and his fear left him.

It was just a touch, but a touch in love.

Neither of us knew what lay ahead.

Neither do you know what is ahead.

Don't worry about that.

Just do the right thing now.

Stay at peace in the grocery line.

Stay at peace with the little things.

Touch someone in love and treat your brother right.

Then you'll be better prepared to handle the big flashes.

It depends on both perspective and preparation.

Whether the big flashes light you up or burn you up.

Where's My Nickel?

=================

I took my wife to Johnny Rockets tonight.

Johnny Rockets is a '40s style hamburger place. It looks just like a burger joint from the '40s and '50s.

I like it because it's pleasantly different, and they have an awesome veggie burger and no-salt fries.
http://www.johnnyrockets.com

They have tabletop jukeboxes at each booth. Only those that are over 30 will remember jukeboxes. True to form, the jukeboxes only take nickels. That's how much it costs to listen to an oldie but goodie song at Johnny Rockets.

When the waiter comes, they leave you two nickels to listen to any two songs on the jukebox.

Whatever you choose, plays over the entire restaurant just like the old-time jukeboxes.

I turned the nostalgic metal tabs that held pages of old songs from the '40s, '50s, '60s and '70s. I settled on two of them.

I searched the table and found one nickel hidden under a napkin. It plopped in the jukebox and I pressed the letter and number matching the song of the past.

I looked for the other nickel and found it behind the veggie burger paper. I plopped the other nickel and heard it reassuringly clink and clank down the ancient mechanism.

The sounds brought back memories of days more mechanical and less computerized. Again I pressed the letter and number for the sound that I hadn't heard for 20 years.

It was a slow time of day and there was only one other table with people in it. I knew the songs would be played in the order selected and perhaps the people at the other table had a couple of songs before mine.

Johnny Rockets continuously has old-time music playing, so again I figured the jukebox automatically played songs until a customer selected songs.

I waited as three songs played and still neither of my two graced my ears.

Puddin began to flip through the song list. Puddin is under 35. I wasn't sure whether she remembered jukeboxes but the mechanism is simple whether you remember how to operate jukeboxes or not.

"Where's my nickel?" she asked.
"Your nickel?"

"I put both nickels in the jukebox," I said.

Puddin didn't seem to mind and began digging in her purse. It sounded like rattling around in a cornflakes box but she triumphantly brought forth a nickel.

She plopped her nickel in and pressed C10.

I looked to see what C10 was. I was curious to see what she wanted to hear. C10 was an Aretha Franklin classic, RESPECT. I remember reading somewhere it was voted in the top ten songs of all time.

My songs still hadn't played.
I waited.

The first song that I had selected was by Van Morrison. I hadn't heard of the song but I really like another Van Morrison song called "Have I Told You Lately" so I wanted to hear the one on the jukebox.

Then I heard a familiar tune.

I heard a familiar voice.

It was the queen of soul, Aretha Franklin singing, "RESPECT."

Puddin had dropped her nickel in less than a minute ago and her song was playing. Mine were nowhere to be heard.

Sometimes the MountainWings Moment comes in an instant. At other times it slowly dawns.

Like the crowd in Johnny Rockets, this was a slow time.

What happened to my songs?

I waited as song after song played, still nothing of my two. Puddin was rumbling in the cornflakes purse again and produced two more nickels. They disappeared into the slot of the jukebox.

Within three or four minutes, her new selections were playing.

The MountainWings Moment flew closer.
The voice got louder, "Where's my nickel?"

It wasn't Puddin's voice, but the voice of the spirit gently whispering. I had taken a nickel that wasn't mine.

The name of the first song Puddin had chosen rang in my spirit.

RESPECT

Sure, I was paying for the dinner and could have said, "Since I am paying for it, both nickels were legally mine," but I knew in higher truth that wouldn't fly.

I had taken a nickel that didn't belong to me.

"Are you sure you pushed the buttons correctly?" Puddin asked.

"Of course I'm sure," I said. "Even if I accidentally pushed the wrong buttons on one song, I sure didn't push the wrong buttons on two songs."

"My songs aren't playing because I took your nickel," I explained.

"But I didn't mind, I didn't even think anything about it," Puddin responded.

She didn't and neither did I but Someone else did. Someone else was watching my actions and immediately brought the consequences to light.

"I was wrong to take your nickel," I said, "that's why my songs aren't playing."

"But you only took one nickel, therefore only one of your songs wouldn't be playing if that were the reason," Puddin explained.

"You don't reap what you sow, you reap the fruit of what you sow. If you plant a seed, you don't reap a seed, you reap a whole plant. It is a spiritual principle that I am being reminded of."

If I wrongfully took one nickel, my penalty is not just one nickels worth.

We ordered dessert. We stayed in Johnny Rockets almost an hour after my first nickel dropped. We had fun and talked like two youths on a date. My songs never played. All of Puddin's did.

Some will say that it was just an odd coincidence, a chance occurrence that had absolutely nothing to do with Puddin's nickel. I can't scientifically disprove those that doubt. Spiritual things are often felt and revealed more than proved.

MountainWings Moments are tenuous, wispy, and grasped only when your perception moves to a new level. Grasped only when blinded eyes and deaf ears are opened.

To someone who doesn't believe such things happen, it's nonsensical gibberish. To me, a scientist, it was obvious cause and effect. But then, all scientists don't agree either.

Most think that a nickel is a small thing.

It is.

But the principle is big. I was being reminded not to be slack in even the small things.

If you will take someone's nickel unjustly, then you might take someone's dime. Then a quarter, then a dollar, then a hundred dollars, then a thousand, then ten thousand, then a million.

The amount is not nearly as important as the principle and the spirit behind it.

RESPECT that which belongs to another, even if it's just a nickel.

If you won't take a nickel unjustly. . .

. . .you can be trusted with a million.

Are you not hearing the music?

Maybe just maybe, you haven't been fair. You haven't
given or shared all that you were supposed to.

Maybe you are legally right but spiritually left.

Maybe just maybe, you need to give someone his or her
five cents worth.

Though I didn't hear the song, I told Puddin "I love you!"
That didn't even cost a nickel, but is worth far more.

Does anyone have to ask you,

Where's my nickel?"

Heavy Ink

=========

I read years ago of the late Whitney Young. He was the president of the Urban League, a civil rights organization. How he handled a particular situation made a lasting impact.

While traveling on a flight in the midst of America's turbulent times of civil rights protest, a passenger recognized him from television.

He approached Mr. Young and said, "I was with you and your organization before you began all of this protesting, but now that you've started that, you no longer have my support."

Whitney Young was unruffled, perhaps accustomed to much criticism in such times. He quickly removed a small blank notepad and pen from his suit pocket and handed it to the man.

He calmly asked, "I would like to present your comments to our board of directors, but I would also like to present your contributions to our cause while you were with us. If you would be so kind as to list the things that you did for us while we had your support, I would greatly appreciate it.

I would like our board to know exactly what we have lost."

Whitney had learned from years of experience and never was the notepad ever filled with so much as a scratch of ink.

I never forgot that simple lesson.

There are times when we are presented with constructive criticism from those who truly wish us well and actively help us to do better.

There are also many other times we will receive comments from those who are simply miffed about a pet peeve of theirs.

They don't know our vision or our purpose.

Maybe there is something they simply don't like or are jealous of and it's a personal thing.

Mr. Young's actions come to mind whenever such situations arise.

Whenever someone says they are leaving, be it my life, the church I pastor, my company, or MountainWings, I have never actually handed them a notepad, but I write their contributions in my mind so I can answer the question,

"What am I really losing?"

So many moan and sulk for years over things and people gone from their lives who would have had an empty notepad.

They made no contribution for the good in your world, only a loud noise as they left.

In many cases, not only would the notepad have been empty, but also they would have stolen the pad.

Don't judge a person's comments or exit from your world solely on whether they've done anything for you, but the ink on that notepad weighs in heavily and should bring you closer to the reality of what you have actually lost.

The Faulty Valve

==============

We recently called a repair company out to fix the icemaker on our refrigerator.

He came and studied the problem and discovered that a valve was faulty. He replaced the valve and after a short while ice was produced. The valve was a small part on the whole refrigerator, but this small part blocked months of ice from coming forth.

It is this same way with life.

One tiny thing in your relationship can stop cubes of joy from being experienced.

Perhaps, it is just the unappreciation of the other person. Many times we don't know what we have until we lose it.

One near-microscopic item in your diet such as crystals of salt can make the difference in the blood throughout your whole body flowing properly.

One mindset change from "I sure can't stand this job" to "I am blessed to have a job after thousands were laid off this month" can make eight hours a day change from drudgery to ease.

Two dollars given to a homeless person with the words "have a special day because you are someone special," without them asking, could change their life forever with the feeling that somebody cares.

One small step of trying an idea that you believe could work may make the difference in you becoming an employer instead of an employee.

What one thing do you need to change in your life to allow the waters of life to flow?

Two dollars given to a homeless person with the words "have a special day because you are someone special," without them asking, could change their life forever with the feeling that somebody cares.

Yes, the above paragraph was repeated.

Go do this. Unstop the valve.

A MountainWings Original
by James Bronner

Dad Dee

========

Dad Dee is the most precious word that I hear.

My two-year-old calls me that.

The odd thing is, it's incorrect.

I am his father, the word and meaning are correct,
just the pronunciation is wrong.

It should be pronounced "Dad e" with the accent on the
first syllable, not the second.

My son pronounces it "Dad Dee" with the accent and an
extra D on the second syllable.

It's absolutely grammatically incorrect.

Yet it is perfect.

You see, it's wrong, but it's right.

It's sincere.

I would rather have a two-year-old mispronouncing the word, but saying it with love, than the most articulate person addressing me with grandiose titles, but a mischievous heart and purpose.

It is better to have someone say "I sho du luv you" and mean it, than to have them eloquently recite, "my dearest, I have admiration, adoration, and emotional depth of feeling for you that my heart cannot contain. Each time the thought of you crosses my mind it echoes upon my trembling lips as I impatiently call your name waiting on your. . ."

You get my drift.

If you have perfect facility of language at your disposal, that's great. I appreciate and prefer fine diction, but I value honesty of heart a million times more.

My two-year-old teaches me each day that all of man's so-called perfection pales in comparison to the pure things of the spirit.

Esteemed father, parental overseer, Mr. Bronner, my beloved parent, most respected and honored father, all of those titles are nice. They reek of respect and position. They have their place.

As I get out of a car that modern technology says is one of the most advanced vehicles on the planet and open the door to the house, I await a voice.

It's a shrill voice. A voice that lacks maturation and the power of masculine bass.

It is a voice that cannot discuss the deeper things of life, technology, business, or worldly events.

It is a voice that would not even understand the concept of MountainWings.

The voice has a very limited vocabulary.
Only a few words grace the lips of the two-year-old.

I am boss over many people at work.
I can look around each day and claim material ownership of much.

That's nice.

All of the world's stuff is nice, but it pales in comparison to that little voice.

When I hear that little voice, with that little incorrectly pronounced word, the whole world stops.

No matter what has transpired that day, that little word sends warmth, joy, and sunshine to make life as bright as a cloudless midsummer's day.

Dad Dee

What's not perfect in your life?

But yet is...

How To Beat Traffic

==================

If you want to beat traffic. . .

Pick some fruit!!

Yesterday it took me an hour and fifteen minutes to go 10 miles.

I was frustrated.
I was powerless.
I was exhausted.
I was grateful.
I was victorious.
I was energized.

Heavy traffic volumes are a fact of life in any big city. Many of the local governments fund road improvement programs only to close lanes as they improve the roads.

Lanes close, traffic increases, people get more frustrated and distracted, they have accidents, they cause more traffic pile-ups.

It's a vicious cycle.

It is often said that a person's first reaction in times of crisis tells a lot about that person. I say that a person's reaction while traveling six inches per minute tells even more about that person.

Sitting in traffic is one of the best times to pick some fruit.

Pick some patience. . .
You'll be able to relax.
After all, you'll be sitting there for a while anyway.

Pick some peace. . .
Try something different --- instead of listening to the radio
traffic reports about the traffic you're sitting in, turn the
radio off. Play a classical CD. Or better yet, just enjoy
the quiet time.

Pick some kindness. . .
Smile at the person in the car next to you.
Now that's really different!

Pick some love. . .
Start a conversation with your spouse or child about
something you know is bothering them. Time spent
driving can be time spent talking and understanding each
other.

Pick some joy. . .
Be thankful that you're not the person involved in the
calamity that's causing the traffic.

Pick some faith. . .
Take this time to look up at the sky, observe the trees,
marvel at the birds. Think about your own life.
Then you'll know for sure that there is a God.

Pick some gentleness. . .
I know you have a cell phone, so pick it up and call
someone you haven't spoken to in months.
You still remember the number.

Pick some goodness. . .
Plan a good deed that you'll do for someone as soon as you get out of the traffic. Maybe there's something you can do immediately to help the person on the side of the road.

Pick some meekness. . .
No matter what kind of car you're riding in, understand that it's not by your own works that you were able to obtain it.

Once you pick your fruit, your frustration, powerlessness, and exhaustion will transform into gratitude, victory and energy.

You'll have a new outlook on life all because you pulled over,

. . . and decided to pick some fruit.

A Mountain Wings Original
by C. Elijah Bronner

Babies Cry More
= = = = = = = = = = = = =

"How's it going Mr. Peterson?"

"It's a dog eat dog world Woody, and I'm wearing Milk Bone underwear."

That's a greeting from Norm on the TV show "Cheers."

All of us have one of those days.
Some of us have one of those seasons.
Some even have one of those lives.

It feels like the world is chewing on us.
It isn't, it just feels that way.

I have long realized that life isn't really what it is,
it's what we think it is based on relative things and our knowledge level.

If you have traveled extensively, you know that in many parts of the world just clean drinking water is a rarity.

We flush with clean drinking water.

So many of us have so much when you compare it.
Those of you who are reading this have access to the net, email, and a computer.

You can see and you are not reading this from a hospital.
We have so much, yet there is an innate tendency to complain.

I tried to think of the easiest point in our lives to see if we complained then.

Babies have perhaps the easiest life around.
Babies don't have to go the toilet because mama changes their diapers. Mama breast feeds them or gives them a bottle, rocks them to sleep, and lets them sleep as much as they want.

Babies go to bed when they want.
Babies wake up when they want.

Babies don't have to work.
Babies don't have to deal with bills or bosses.
Babies don't worry if their thighs have gotten too fat or if their hair is receding.

It's as easy as it gets.

With all of that, babies cry more.

Babies cry more, with all of that.

Maybe it's not circumstances, but the closer we are to babies (regardless of circumstances) the more we cry and complain.

I shall leave you with that thought.

Babies cry more.

With all of that.

The Stranger
= = = = = = = = = = =

Today I had a MountainWings Moment.

It is really amazing that once you begin to open your mind and spirit to new ideas how you become elevated to another level with each situation that you encounter.

I recently read the MountainWings issue about running the hill or allowing the hill to run you and it immediately came to mind after my recent encounter with a stranger.

Today, I had an errand to run during work. The errand involved driving in downtown Atlanta during lunchtime, which I rarely do.

I got lost trying to find my way back to the interstate.

Nevertheless, upon leaving the downtown area, I was making a left turn through an intersection where there was a crosswalk.

I saw a man walking in the crosswalk as I began to turn, apparently, he didn't see me coming. He looked as if I had startled him and as if he thought that I was going to strike him with my car.

The man just stopped dead in his tracks. Since I was in the middle of the intersection blocking the road and he had stopped walking, I proceeded through the crosswalk instead of allowing this man to pass first.

As I slowly drove by, the man yelled out, "You stupid b_____."

I looked into my rearview mirror and watched him cross the street.

I was totally shocked.
I thought that his words were certainly out of line.

For a moment, I began to let his words penetrate my spirit as I took them personally. I was torn between shouting out to him "Go to h____" or "Jesus loves you."

All of a sudden, I had another thought; it was like a light bulb flooding every corner of my mind. I immediately recalled the story about running up the hill.

I knew that this was a MountainWings Moment.

This was a lesson that I had to learn. I would have to learn how to handle negativity from anyone, stranger or friend. I would have to learn to control my emotions when someone says or does something that I don't feel is warranted.

I know some may think that I am making far too much of this scenario; that it wasn't that serious but you'll be surprised how a small negative comment can have a big impact if you don't climb the mountain.

I have become a more open-minded person; I often see things in their fullness. I feel that there is purpose for everything that happens in my life, although that purpose may not always be revealed at the exact moment a situation occurs.

I know this may sound strange to some, but I am now learning to find the good in things that happen in my life.

I've decided to weed through all things in the garden of life that I may first consider bad and try to find some light or some goodness in it, even if it is microscopic.

I guess the words of that stranger were not in vain; they taught me another little lesson for that day and let me climb a little higher on the mountain.

by Britte Blair, Assistant to Nathaniel Bronner

Grandma in Jamaica
=================

On our second day in Jamaica, we had the typical tourist's day minus the ganja and a few other things.

We practiced some basic principles of surviving temptation island.

You're saying, "but you are in Jamaica, that's different. That's a different culture and a different latitude. It's different over there."

No it isn't.

It's the same thing, it's just a little more direct and no one knows in Jamaica.

You'll be surprised what people will do when they don't think anyone back at home will find out. Many people who walk the beach topless in Jamaica would never do that at a beach where people they knew frequented.

Rule #1 of temptation island:
Behave as if someone you admire and respect is watching you.

Whether you know it or not, someone is watching. Behavior is different based on who's looking.

There is a saying that you should always dance like no one's watching. You should dance, sing, and play like no one is watching. There are some things you should let yourself go at.

There are other things where you need to keep yourself. If you let yourself go, someone will catch you whose hands are not too clean.

In Jamaica, as on all temptation islands, you need to dance like someone is watching.

There is a good rule of thumb that I always counsel people with. It's simple and it helps them to stay out of trouble. It's the watching rule.

Do I tell them to behave as if God is watching? No.

Many have no idea what, who, why, where or even if God exists. That's too nebulous for many.

I tell them this:
Act as if you would have to tell your grandmother what you did each day.

The vast majority can relate to that. They may have questions about God, but they know about Grandma. Most Grandmas are good. Most grandchildren don't want to disappoint Grandmas.

Grandma was holding up fine until the one in the purple bikini waltzed by and winked.

Rule #2 of Temptation Island tomorrow.

Purple Bikini

=============

Our 2nd day in Jamaica, Temptation Island.

"What would grandma think about this?" is always a good
question to ask yourself to keep yourself out of trouble.
We had grandma, wives, mother, and a church
congregation to think about.

That was working fine until the one in the purple bikini
waltzed by and winked. Did she really wink? I don't
know but it had the same effect.

She didn't just walk by, she sauntered by. She knew she
was being watched and wanted to make absolutely sure
of it.

Slowly and deliberately she stepped while the three
ministers lay in the sun.

She blocked our sun for a brief moment as she caused a
minor eclipse.

Did you see that my brother asked?
"See what?" I responded.
My wife reads MountainWings.

Since he called the phenomenon blocking the sun to my attention, out of scientific curiosity I turned my head to observe.

She daintily stepped into the water as if on stage. She never really swam. She just went into the very warm water waist deep, turned around a few times and then got out.

She walked in front of us again. She had a huge grin on her face. It was actually more like a smirk.

She knew she was well-proportioned and would throw most men's minds and hormones into a frenzy.

Little did she realize that we were thinking about Grandma.

The brother in the middle never said a word. The younger one then quoted rule #2 on temptation island:

"You can't flirt, talk, or even look too hard at something tempting."

Your temptation island may be a refrigerator. You can't walk by, open the door, and stare at the half a gallon of cherry vanilla ice cream that's your favorite.

You can't challenge it. It has patience. You have desire.

If you stare at it, you not only have desire but a good degree of stupidity as well.
Don't flirt with something that's tempting.

Even a simple, "hot out here isn't it?" can start you down the wrong road.

Remember this:

With all temptations, you can never fall if you never take the first step.

Trying to stand and face off with something that is highly desirable is not a good idea. You will never prove how strong you are.

You will only find out where your breaking point is, even ministers.

I thought about Grandma and stared at the beautiful waves.

The ocean waves.

Then I smelled it and an old familiar desire came flooding back.

Tomorrow, rule #3 on temptation island.

A Little Chicken

===============

I smelled it and an old familiar desire came flooding back.

Jamaica is known for the assaults on the senses.

It's bright, hot, loud, and many smells fill the air.

Jamaica has one world famous food.

Jerk Chicken.

I smelled jerk chicken.

I had not eaten jerk chicken since I was last in Jamaica. That was over ten years ago. Not only had I not had any jerk chicken in ten years, I hadn't had any chicken at all.

I don't eat chicken.

That's a health thing. I was completely vegetarian for many years until I recently started eating the meat that Jesus ate. I started eating certain types of fish. The only meat that I had eaten for the last ten years was fish.

Jerk chicken tastes different from American chicken. The Jamaicans cook it in roadside barrels and the charcoal smoke drifts all the way to the beach. It's spiced and flavored to perfection.

My brother wanted jerk chicken. He had no such restrictions on his diet. Chicken, and plenty of it, was fine by him.

Temptation Island Rule #3:
Be careful whom you associate with, sooner or later you will be drawn to behave the same way.

My brother never tried to entice me to eat the jerk chicken. There really isn't that much wrong with eating Jamaican chicken. My diet is a personal choice.
My brother is very healthy and has an extremely healthy diet. Chicken, especially jerk chicken, just happens to be on his menu.

All of us went to the jerk chicken barrel. You are literally enveloped in the savory smoke as it waifs from the barrel They don't give you slices of bread. They actually slice the bread from a solid loaf.

"Give me extra bread with extra sauce," my brother asked The cook complied.

My brother carried his prize eagerly to the room.
He had a full chicken.

The chicken seemed to disappear between his teeth as if it were simply melting when it touched his lips.
My other brother, who eats as I do, watched the feast.

Pausing between bites long enough to push a good bit of chicken to my other brother he said, "I ordered extra chicken and extra bread; I won't be able to eat all of this."

My brother stared at the chicken while the chicken stared at him.

"A little chicken won't hurt," he said and soon the chicken

as melting in his mouth.

hat left me hungry and chickenless, staring at two
others in chicken heaven.

 little chicken won't hurt," I said.

mptation Island Rule #3:
 careful whom you associate with, sooner or later you
ill be drawn to behave the same way.

Three Things

===========

On our recent Jamaican vacation, surviving the temptation island of Jamaica was very similar to surviving the everyday life of America.

The three rules that I gave in the previous MountainWings paralleled my grandmother's rules of life.

1. Work Hard   2. Be Honest 3. Keep Good Company

She told my father this over 70 years ago.

It still applies.

Work hard, be honest and keep good company.

Labor Saving

============

"The economic and technological triumphs of the past few years have not solved as many problems as we thought they would, and in fact, have brought us new problems we did not foresee."
Henry Ford II

What if you had to wash clothes by hand?

What if you had no vacuum cleaner?

What if you had to light a fire and wait for a pot-bellied iron stove to warm up before you could cook?

What if you had to ride a horse or walk?

What if you had to walk to your best friend's house to talk?

What if you had to write by hand instead of using a computer?

What if you had to heat your bathwater with a fire in a tin tub?

What if you had to light a candle instead of flicking a light switch?

What if you had to get your food from the garden instead of the grocery store?

What if you had to read a book instead of getting it from TV?

We have tons of time and labor saving devices.

Yet, we have less free time now than ever.

We have atomic clocks that are accurate to the millisecond.

The clocks set themselves and save us the time and trouble.

Though we can tell time far more accurate, we seem to have far less of it.

As much as ancestors had to do, shortly after dark, they went to bed. Often, we are just getting started after dark.

Maybe we need to turn off our labor saving devices for a while, so that we can get some rest.

Learning to Run
=============

The two-year-old likes to run.

It warms my heart when I see his funny movements as he runs.

It also scares me because young children have a tendency to fall very easily.

I was out shopping with my sons when the two-year-old started to run.

He fell.

If you are a parent, you completely understand the phrase, "it hurts you more than it does them." There is something that pains worse than physical torment to see your little one hurt.

He skinned his knee and elbow. He cried for a few minutes and finally with the soothing of Daddy, quieted down.

We are like my two-year-old.

There are so many areas of life where we must run:
some by choice, some by the force of circumstances.

There are so many new things.
There are so many times when our steps are unsure and
we are not experienced runners.

The older I get, the more I understand how a Divine
Father can let us go through some things and fall. I was
tempted to stop my son when I saw him run. I knew
that sooner or later, if not that day then one day,
he would fall.

I also knew that if he was to ever learn how to run,
he must fall, and often I had to watch him do it.

I fell in business several times before I was able to run.

I fell in relationships several times before I had sense
enough to stop looking for perfection and know that we
all have faults.

Even your second child is reared differently from the first
because you learn some things from falling with that first
one.

I fell off of my bicycle.
I fell off of my motorcycle.
I fell on skates (roller and ice).
I even choked a few times while learning to swim.

We often fall when learning to run the things of life.

Too often, bruises stop us from ever trying to run again.
We are afraid that we will slip and get hurt.
We are afraid of the pain.

My son runs much better now. I still wince when I see
him run on a hard surface, but he won't stop running.

At only two, he has one of the keys of life.

He won't stop running just because he fell.

Your bruises will heal, you will get up, and the path will
still be there.

Though at times you may not think it so,
the Divine Father is still watching over you.

He just knows that He has to let you fall,
if you are ever to learn to run.

The Good OLD Days?
==================

People talk about the good old days.

Life was good, life had less stress, and life didn't have the pollution, the crime, the violence, the drugs, and the fears and turmoil of modern life.

It was the good old days,

... or was it?

One of the measures of all of the above is simply how long you've lived. Sure, lifespan is not everything but it is a good relative measuring tool. All of the above factors take it's toll in shortened lifetimes.

With increased pollution, you should die sooner.
With increased crime, you should die sooner.
With increased stress, you should die sooner.
With increased drug use, you should die sooner.

Many measuring standards change, years don't.
Money does.

Five dollars now is not five dollars twenty years ago.

You will have to make adjustments to compare a dollar now against a dollar twenty years ago.

Time is constant (well almost, there is relativity to consider and the speed variations with stellar movement and

their effect on time but that's not important for this
discussion).

A second is still a second.
A minute is still a minute.

An hour is still an hour. A day is still a day. And a year
is still a year, whether you are talking about now or a
hundred or a thousand years ago.

You would think that we lived much longer in the good
OLD days. It looks like I even remember a lot more older
folk when I was very young.

These are the average life spans in the U. S. since 1900
according to The Dept. of Health and Human Services.

Year	Male	Female
1900	48.2	51.1
1940	60.8	65.2
1950	65.6	71.1
1960	66.6	73.3
1970	67.1	74.7
1980	70.0	77.4
1990	71.8	78.8
1996	73.0	79.0

Based on these figures, we are living about three months
longer each year since 1900.

The more time passes, the longer we live, even with all of
the seeming negatives of the modern world.

Sure, there is a lot wrong with the world, but maybe there was more wrong back then.

Maybe the good OLD days weren't all that good and maybe today isn't all that bad.

It's a matter of both knowledge and perspective.

I'm glad to be living in the good NEW days, there are more of them.

March 4th
= = = = = = = = =

During college, my favorite television show was Star Trek.

The opening theme in Star Trek was:

'Space: The Final Frontier. These are the voyages of the starship Enterprise. It's five-year mission: To explore strange new worlds... To seek out new life and new civilizations...

To Boldly Go Where No Man Has Gone Before."

Captain Kirk spoke that. Captain James Tiberius Kirk.

He was a fictional character but a real type of spirit.

We all have a final frontier and it is not in space, at least not outer space. It's in inner space. That's where all of the real battles are fought. That's where the real untamed territory is. That's where the greatest victories and defeats happen.

Far too often, we stay within confining walls that we think are safe, but actually, they are just a prison.

Dreams will never be realized without risks.
Love will never be experienced without exposure.
You can't even help another person without risking being hurt yourself.

The more people we reach with MountainWings, the

more we help. Always among each new few thousands, there is someone unbalanced and filled with hate who will lash out at us. It's a risk.

Inner and outer space has dangers.

So many wish for things that are never achieved.

Love, financial security, good health, peace of mind, even just a good night's sleep are things that often elude many for life.

Mike Murdock put it like this:

"If you want something you've never had, you've got to do something you've never done."

You've got to boldly go where you've never gone before.

One definition of a fool is a person who keeps doing the same thing and expecting different results.

We often stand on the dock but are afraid to launch out into the deep. Afraid to go into space, afraid to move, afraid to speak, even afraid to dance.

If you want something you've never had...

Do you?

Want something you've never had.

If so, then maybe today is the perfect day to start.

Why today?
Because it's March 4th.

March forth on March 4th.

Boldly go where you've never gone before.

You've got new life to discover.

March Forth!

(This issue was sent on March 4th but today is as good a day as any to march forth. You don't have to wait on March 4th.)

One Week
=========

This is a true story.

It happened to one of the people who work for me, the writer of MountainWings.com.

Last week, a young man in the shipping department asked to take some time off from work. His wife's grandmother had passed and he and his family were driving up north to the funeral.

She passed on the 8th of this month.

I talked with the young man today and asked him how things went.

"You know we went to the funeral for my wife's grandmother and while we were there, her grandfather died also. She died on the 8th and he died on the 14th. He died 20 minutes after the viewing of the body at the funeral home. They buried them both at the same funeral, and they buried them in the same grave, one on top of the other."

They had been married over 50 years.

The events had the appearance of tragedy, yet I saw something greater. The shortest MountainWings issue of recent times was a simple quote.

This was the quote:

"If you live to be a hundred, I want to live to be a hundred minus one day, so that I never have to live without you."

That's real marriage. That's real love. It's stuff that most will only read about in romance novels. Few live it, few feel it, fewer still would die for it.

Few people realize that to truly achieve a love like that, you do have to die. You have to die to self.

The grandfather simply couldn't make it one week without his love. Or maybe, she had already said to him:

"If you live to be a hundred, I want to live to be a hundred minus one week, so that I never have to live a week without you."

An Honest Response
=================

A comment from a MountainWings subscriber:

Sometimes, I can't stand to read your site because there has never been a time when I didn't get a tug at my heart when I read it. What I read is exactly what I needed to read. I just DO NOT feel like having to follow through with the action that this site always suggests to my heart.

Often, when the time comes to do the "right thing," we really don't feel like doing it. We usually do the things that we feel like doing without prompting .

I always feel like eating something sweet, but I need prompting and knowledge for that raw salad.

At MountainWings, I strive to remind you of the "right things" to do. I know you don't always feel like it.

Guess what? Neither do I.

We all do NOT feel like doing the right things at times.

It is the constant battle between heart and flesh, between others' needs and our wants, between instant gratification and disciplined development, and between doing what's right and what feels really good right now.

That's the battle.

That's also the mission.

Tired of Waiting
= = = = = = = = = = = = =

I have been a widower for 6 years today; I need a helpmate in my life. I think God has a perfect mate for me out there, but I am tiring of waiting.
I don't know what to do.

The above was a prayer request sent to MountainWings. We rarely publish prayer requests but this one struck me.

So many are tired of waiting.

Tired of waiting on a mate.
Tired of waiting on a financial breakthrough.
Tired of waiting to get well.
Tired of waiting to retire.
Tired of waiting to...

You name it and we are tired of waiting on it.

A bit of advice for those who don't know what to do.

Change your type of waiting on.

Huh?

Change your type of waiting on.

Waiting on has two essential meanings.

1. To pause in expectation.
2. To serve another.

The majority follows definition #1.

We pause in expectation of something happening,
something coming our way.

... love coming our way.
... money coming our way.
... deliverance coming our way.
... happiness coming our way.
... healing coming our way.

Usually, we can't speed up those things with current
circumstances. We do the best we can and still it lingers
and appears as if it will never come.

We may not be able to easily expedite those things
coming our way, but we can IMMEDIATELY wait on
someone else.

We can serve others.

We can be a friend to the lonely, though they may not be
able offer us anything in return.

We can help others financially, though our own finances may be in a wreck. I have found with giving and helping that it is usually far more a matter of spirit than resources.

Even within the church, those with the largest incomes give the smallest percentage.

Though you may be struggling, there are many in worse condition and even 25 cents to a hungry person is a big blessing.

We are often lonely because we are often idle.

When you are busy, you generally aren't lonely.

Wait on... be a servant.

Don't wait on a thing, you be the waiter who brings the thing.

"Whoever would be the greatest,
must be the servant of all."
Mark 10:44

Wait In Peace
============

Yesterday, I told you about my Jeep battery and the trickle effect.

I had to wait 15 minutes while the battery charged enough to start the car.

I took those 15 minutes of delay and used the time to clean out the Jeep.

There are always times when waiting is necessary: in a long grocery store line, in a restaurant, in a bank line, in a doctor's office, even while a slow web page is loading.

Life gives us delays.

Most of those times, people fuss and complain about the delay.

One of the measures of the growth of your spirit is patience.

Learn to do this: If you can't speed it up, shut up.

Shut up, relax, read a book, whistle a tune, or softly sing to yourself (yes, people will look at you strangely but your peace will calm them).

My late father was a very busy and successful man. He worked hard but understood the great value of peace and managed to find a slice of it whenever he could.

When he found an opportunity (or when the opportunity found him) to be quietly still, he took it.

In such a busy and hectic world he told me this, "son, with all of the things that you do, learn to grab peace and rest whenever you can, never stand up if you can sit down and never sit down if you can lay down."

That was good advice. I now understand he was speaking more spiritually than physically but it applies to both realms.

Do you have a song to sing or whistle, or a book to read the next time a peaceful opportunity of delay finds you?

Wait in Peace.

Pick Thee Me Up

=================

Pick Thee Me Up

That's another one of Josees' expressions.

Josees is my two-year-old son.

He doesn't have perfect syntax. Even that simple statement requires an ear trained in babyonics to understand.

Pick thee me up!

He says it as he stands in front of me with his outstretched arms and a pleading in his eyes and voice.

Pick thee me up!
Pick thee me up!
Pick thee me up!

Over and over he pleads until sooner or later he's picked up, giving both of us relief.

He is smart enough to recognize the father.

He is smart enough to know that the father can lift him out of his situation.

He is smart enough to keep pleading until his plea is heard.

Whenever he is frustrated, whenever he is afraid, whenever he feels alone, whenever he needs rest, whenever he needs, he asks the father to "Pick thee me up."

It is a lesson that we all would do well to learn, for we all have a heavenly father.

We all, sooner or later need to call upon him.

We all need to say. . .

Pick thee me up!

Josees was named after Joses, the brother of Jesus.

There were times when Jesus had to call on his father, and say, "Pick thee me up."

So will you.

(1 Cor 6:14) And God hath both raised up the Lord, and will also raise up us by his own power.

Pick Thee Me Up

Then What?
==========

What if you won the lottery?

What if you won a big one, like 100 million dollars or so?

What would you do?

Let's go down the usual list.

Pay off the home (no make that buy a mansion - cash).
Buy several exotic cars
Buy clothes
Travel to exotic places
Hire servants (maids, chefs and chauffeurs)
Take care of relatives (mama at a minimum)
Invest

Then what?

What do you mean "Then What?"
I hear many of you asking, "isn't that enough?"

You see people, it's the "then what" stuff that makes the
real difference in life. All of the stuff on the above list,

you will get tired of in six months.
The excitement will wear off.

You will get bored. People will be after you for your money. You will get paranoid.

You will discover relatives that you didn't know existed or at least you hadn't heard from in years.

They all will want one thing and it won't be your companionship.

So, you will get paranoid, as everyone wants your money.

Then what?

We often make the mistake of assuming that money will solve all of our problems. Money will only solve money problems.

In my experience in business and in ministry, I usually find that it's the "other stuff" that's the real problem, not money.

Often the "other stuff" is the reason for the money problems.

Let's start with the list of what you would do if you won a big lottery and I want to show you how you can live just as happy (if not happier) without the big lottery win.

Pay off the home (no make that buy a mansion – cash).

A house is NOT a home. Many have houses but not homes.

Many have mansions but not homes.

You can't buy a home, only a house.

A home is made with love, friendship, and loyalty.

You can't buy those either.

You can get that without a big cash influx.

Buy several exotic cars.

I have a fairly fancy car now but it pales in comparison to my first car. A Corvair. Not a Corvette, a 1966 Corvair. That was the car Ralph Nader got pulled because it was unsafe. I paid $125.00 for it. It leaked a trail of oil wherever it went. It smoked. It jerked. It might not get you where you intended to go, but it was mine. It was exotic. I got more thrill from that Corvair than from my fancy car now. Exotic is in the mind. Notice the hot graphics on the bus you are riding? Exotic is in the mind.

Buy clothes

A friend of mind saw Stephen Spielberg in a bookstore.

Spielberg is the big movie producer of many of the all time great Hollywood movies.

Spielberg is worth hundreds of millions, if not billions.

He was dressed in shorts, tennis shoes with no socks, and a floppy hat. You can afford to look like multi-millionaire Stephen Spielberg.

Is that exotic enough for you?

Travel to exotic places

There are still a world of things in my city that I have
never seen. Places that I have never walked. Streets that
I have never driven. People that I have never met.
So it is with your city. If you are not happy in your city,
you won't find happiness on top of some foreign
mountain or in some posh village.

Hire servants (maids, chefs and chauffeurs)
Invite your little niece or nephew over and pay them a
toy to help you clean up. That will liven up your day.

Take care of relatives (mama at a minimum)
If your parents or grandparents are still alive, I can
guarantee that they want to talk with you more than you
talk with them. Talk costs you nothing but time and you
don't have to win the lottery to have that. They want a
little of your time, not a new house. Take care of them.

Invest
No matter how little (or much) you earn, always put
something aside. I have seen that saving is a habit that's
not dependent on income but on discipline.

The things that you do after the "then what?" will
ultimately be more important than your list if you won
100 million dollars.

If you've understood this,
congratulations on winning the big one.

Remember the Power of A Smile

================================

I placed the items on the moving belt.

Slowly my packages moved towards the cash register.

The cashier was tired.

I could see it on her face.

It was towards the end of her shift. She had no doubt
been standing and ringing the cash register all day.
I know the cash registers don't ring anymore, they are
computerized, but when I worked as a cashier, they rang.

So she rang the cash register.

I am sure she had duties to perform when she arrived
home.

Even punching the clock would not likely stop the work.

My two-year-old son, Josees, was with me.

She performed her job with all of the speed tired muscles
and weary spirit could summon.

Josees stood in front of the belt across from her.

His tiny frame was inches below the top of the moving belt.

I don't know what made him move away from me and stand there.

Children can at times move more on instinct than logic.

He stood there looking up, sensing something.

She looked down.

"Oh my God, look at that smile!" she exclaimed.

She changed. The tiredness left. The dreariness left.
She appeared as fresh as if she had just walked through the door.

Josees continued standing and smiling.
She continued to be revived.

It was a MountainWings Moment.

I saw not the power of a child, but the power of a pure smile.

You have the same power.

Each day you will meet someone who is tired, weary, and dreary.

Remember, you have the power of a smile.

For many, the first tired, weary, and dreary person you will meet will be in the mirror.

Even in the mirror, the power of a smile still works.

When you have a huge smile, the muscles of your face contract on a special gland in the brain that releases a hormone in the brain that eases stress and causes a slight euphoric high.

Is that true?

I don't know but that's sure what it feels like in my brain.

Smile real big right now and see if that gland is in your brain too.

She was still bubbling as we walked out of the store.

Josees never said a word. He only smiled.

Remember Josees when you meet your weary person each day.

Remember the power of a smile.

Remember you have it.

Remember someone needs it.

Remember.

Keep Hugging
= = = = = = = = = = = =

On rare occasions, a personal answer sent from an advice
or prayer request will be used in a MountainWings issue
when it may help others. This is one of those occasions.

Hi MountainWings,
Here lately I've been torn into a thousand (what feels like
irreplaceable) parts.

To start with, I'm a very emotional person, plus I have a
tender heart for just about everything. I'm a choir
member in high school and I have a golden heart for
choir but also for the friends I've made in choir.

One thing I enjoy doing to my choir friends is showing
them I care by being somewhat affectionate. I don't kiss
anyone but hug them. It's just something I'm so used to
because at my church I do it all the time and nobody says
anything about it. So I'm used to it and comfortable with
it.

Well, just recently I got turned in to the administration for
hugging. Then the other day, I was giving my close
friend a hug and he didn't move. He told me he
generally doesn't give out hugs. I reminded him that it
was strange. He said that when he and I went
ice-skating one time, he accepted two hugs that I offered,
but now he isn't going to hug me.

MountainWings, I'm giving up.

I'm seriously on the verge of giving up my life.
I'm throwing my arms up in the air and saying that I give
up on caring for people. I always feel like if I could just
leave this earth, the choir wouldn't have to worry about
me and neither would he.

I know this is going to land me in hell, but I really feel I
don't know what else to do. What worries me is that
sometimes I'll go to bed each school night and pray to
God, and I'll wake up the next day to find that my prayer
either wasn't answered or it just made my life that much
worse.

I don't mean to say this, but I give up on prayer too.
I totally give up on myself. I would email all those whom
I care about, but the email that I want to send them,
I fear they will turn in to the administration again.

That's why again, I'm throwing up my arms and saying
"Alright that's it!" If I have to live one more day to see
this, I don't think I'll make it to see graduation.

A MountainWings Subscriber, female and in high school

Having a "tender heart" for people has its risks.
Without exception, some people will reject you and let
you down.

When you read the Bible, it's the story of God and Jesus.
Think about it and the rejection They received.

As a pastor of a church and the writer of MountainWings, I reach out to a lot of people. I don't receive a salary or any monetary compensation at the church. I do it for the love of God and the love of people.

MountainWings doesn't receive nearly enough in donations to pay the expenses. Only about 1 in 7,000 send a donation.

Many are appreciative, but most take it for granted. Thus is the path of the servant, understand this.

About 4,000 people join MountainWings each day, yet there are about 500 who leave daily. Sometimes those who leave write very nasty comments giving all types of reasons with all types of misconceptions.

I am often tempted to email them back to either explain or just vent. I will tell you what God told me.

"Let them go and waste no time nor effort, spend all of your energy on those who remain and freely accept what you give."

You will always have those who reject hugs, who reject love, who reject compassion, who reject the good that you do.

Parents will have children who reject them, no matter how hard they try.

Teachers will have students who reject them, no matter how hard they try.

Good Samaritans will have those whom they try to help reject them.

God made a great sacrifice, and yet most of the world rejected His sacrifice then and now.

Your situation is not unusual; it is the path of the servant.

Don't let those who don't appreciate what you are trying to do discourage you.

I often say before each sermon, before each issue of MountainWings, if this can help just one person, it's worth it.

Yes, I know some will reject it but this may not be meant for everyone, it's special.

Even though there are those who have and will continue to reject your hugs, there is one waiting, in desperate need of your hug.

Your hug may save his or her life and world.

Don't let people discourage you. Keep hugging, keep loving, keep giving, it is the way of the servant.

(Mark 10:43-45 NIV) "Not so with you. Instead, whoever wants to become great among you must be your servant, and whoever wants to be first must be slave of all. For even the Son of Man did not come to be served, but to serve, and to give His life as a ransom for many."

Bubbles

========

I stood on my grandmother's front porch with my son. He had a bottle of bubbles. You know the type, it's basically soapy water with a plastic loop on each end. You dip the loop in the bottle, pull it out, and blow it to make bubbles.

My son understood the principle but was vainly trying to blow bubbles. He would dip and dip and blow and blow, but alas, no bubbles.

He handed me the bottle and loop and asked me, "Daddy can you make bubbles?" I hadn't blown bubbles in years.

I am a chemist by education, fairly well-trained in surfactant technology. I have formulated several shampoos, so I understand surface tension and related foaming characteristics of surfactants. Surfactant is just a big fancy word for a soap or detergent.

All that knowledge isn't worth a hoot when trying to blow bubbles from a loop filled with soapy water. I was having no more success than my son. I would dip and puff, no bubbles; the soapy film on the loop would just pop without releasing any bubbles.

After several futile attempts, I changed tactics. Instead of puffing on the loop of soapy water, I gently breathed on it. My son squealed with delight as a big beautiful bubble emerged and floated away.

He grabbed the loop, dipped and blew. No bubbles. I explained to him, "son you can't blow hard, you must ever so gently breathe on the loop to make bubbles."

He restrained his ardent desire to make big bubbles by blowing hard and followed my advice.

Big bubbles.

It was a MountainWings Moment as I saw another principle of life floating away in the bubbles.

There are some things that you can get with brute force, but there are other things that only come with the gentleness of a soft breath.

Too often, we try to force love or real respect. It won't come. It just pops before the bubble can ever form because we try to put too much force on it.

The closer something is to higher spirit, the more it is like bubbles; it can't be forced and is more often found in the soft things of life.

You have a bottle of bubbles and you have been puffing trying to get them out.

Blow beautiful bubbles, breathe easy.

The More
You Do

===============

Where do you get the time?

Someone came to my house today who receives MountainWings.

They said, "I really enjoy MountainWings but where do you get the time to write it?"

They know that I run two businesses, President of one and Executive V. P. of another. Both are substantial businesses and substantial responsibilities.

I am also the Pastor of a church.

I also have a family (that may be the more demanding job).

They wanted to know, where did I get the time to write MountainWings?

There is one point that I want you to understand, "The more you do, the more you can do."

There is an old adage that goes, "If you want something done, give it to a busy person."

By normal logic this would seem backwards. It would appear that if you want to get something done you should give it to someone who has plenty of free time on their hands, someone whose schedule is open, someone with little responsibility and ample room for more.

That would be the normal logic. The truth is the reverse.

If you want something done, give the job to someone who is already doing a lot. Don't give it to someone who has a lot of free time on their hands and is just doing enough to get by.

Let me give you some simple examples.

Who do you find in educational classes that are beyond mandatory or college?

Check that crowd, it will usually be those with a lot of knowledge already.

Go to a gym in July. Don't go at the beginning of the year, you'll mostly find the New Year's resolution crowd that will be long gone in two months.

Who will you find that exercises the most and the hardest?

It will usually be those who are already in shape and who NEED the exercise the least. Those who exercise the most are able to exercise even more. Those who are sedentary get softer and softer and are able to do less and less.
Go to a finance seminar. I'm not talking about a multi-level marketing get rich quick seminar but a real honest

financial seminar on how to handle, invest and make more money. Who will you find? Generally you will find those who are already handling their money far better than average and have far more than average.

There is a simple spiritual principle that reads,

"To those that have they shall get more added to them. To those that don't have, even what they seem to have will be taken away from them." Jesus said that, not me.

I didn't say it but I understand it. I majored in chemistry. It's called Markonikov's law in Chemistry.

The law is about hydrogen atoms and the carbon molecules that unattached hydrogen atoms move to. Markonikov's law states, "them that has gits." The free hydrogen atoms go to the carbons that already have the most hydrogen atoms.

The world puts it this way, "the rich get richer and the poor get poorer." It's always been and will always be that way whether you like it or not.

You may not think it's fair but it's the way it is and will be. The thing is, it doesn't apply just to money. It applies to anything.

Anything!
Those who have an abundance of it already have a much greater probability of getting more than someone who doesn't have any.
You name it: love, money, sex, health, peace, confidence, spiritual enlightenment, etc., it applies.

Anything

That also holds true for the negative things.

Those who are rich in negative things get even more negative things.

So why am I harping on that?

To simply tell you this. . . GET BUSY!!!

When you start doing more, more things will come to you. If you only do what the average does, you will get what the average gets. That makes sense doesn't it?

SO GET BUSY!!!

Remember, the average person never reaches the mountaintop because you can't get to the mountaintop on average effort.

You have to get busy.

Watch This!

=============

Watch This!

It's my sons' favorite words, both the two and five-year-old.

They will often holler out just before they perform some stunt, put a block in place, ride the tricycle in a circle, drive a race car on the video screen, form a letter, read a word, touch their toes, tie their shoes, eat a piece of broccoli, turn a light on, turn a light off, put a plastic liner in the trash can put trash in the trash can, and a thousand other things.

I had a MountainWings Moment during a "Watch This" episode.

I realized that we never stop saying, "Watch This."

Children use "Watch This" to get attention or to gratify themselves that someone notices, admires, appreciates and cares about them. As we age, our methods change but the "Watch This" continues.

Far too many teenagers get in trouble not because they really seek the trouble, nor because they are afraid their parents will find out. They are counting on their parents finding out.

People get married to spite their parents.
It's a "Watch This."

Much of our debt is because we were trying to say, "Watch This."

See what I've: got - done - built
See what I: drive - earn - wear
See whom I: date - am friends with - know

Watch This

Many of our problems stem from self-esteem, either too much or too little. It causes us to focus too much on the "Watch This" phenomenon.

When I saw it in my sons, I tried to recognize it in me.

It was there.

No one can completely get rid of "Watch This," but when you recognize it, you can handle it better.

Now whenever I do something, I ask,
"Is this a 'Watch This' or do I have a pure motive?"

Children and adults use "Watch This" to get attention or to gratify themselves that someone notices, admires, appreciates and cares about them.

Remember the phrase, "Dance like nobody's watching?"

Maybe we should live like nobody's watching,

except from heaven.

Courage

========

Look, I've never written anything like this before so please forgive my "roughness."

We spent the last twenty plus years watching every walk of life kill, maim, steal, torture, lie, and every form of hideous death from babies to holy men.

It all culminated in my wife dying in my arms from medical incompetence recently which resulted in my financial devastation and loss of all physical possessions, friends, and family.

Over middle age, broke and living in an alley shack, I write this...

I'm wondering how did one of the highest awarded police officers in this country come to this end?

In the darkness, an old friend I'd not heard from for years sent me a forwarded email containing your site.

I went there and I opened the area you offer for "past issues" and I started reading.

I look around my walls hung with medals and hundreds of awards from our country's president, senate, state governor, halls of fame, children groups, grateful families, fellow officers, etc.
But I feel empty.

I've saved so many lives and put my life on the line for strangers in scenarios where I knew I would and should have died...but didn't. Our President gave me the highest award in our country in law enforcement for one of those acts.

But when it mattered most, no one would take my life to save my partner's. Oh how I begged.

I failed her.

In this blackness alone, it wasn't what I read exactly. It was you offering the words, making the effort to reach out to total strangers.

It finally dawned on me about courage. I have the medals and awards for many acts of bravery, but you folks are awarded something much more honorable... the grace to bestow courage when all is lost.

Thank you for what you do and this priceless gift I've just received from your heart

...the courage to go on.

From this dark pit of hell, please hear one weak voice that lost his faith in so much evil.

Thank you for what you do. Maybe it was all worth it if there are people like you.

God bless you all.
J.S. Everett, Washington

Our reply to J.S. from MountainWings:
If you were there for her, you didn't fail her.

For all who have lost loved ones, go to
www.AirJesus.com and listen to the message,
"One Hour and 40 Minutes."

J.S.'s reply:

The doctor wept at our side.
He'd never heard a death rattle say, "I love you" softly.

It would be my honor, gratitude to you all and a loving
memory to all the lives this wonderful person's spirit has
touched. You have my permission to publish this.

I was at her side for six years fighting; you're the first to
ever mention that.

This time I believe she held me through the tears.

I believe you people are being 'guided.'

Thank you,
J.S.

The Diaper
==========

"Why didn't you change his diaper?" my wife somewhat caustically asked.

"You left with the kids at 10:30 this morning, it's 2:30 and Josees diaper hasn't been changed.

Why didn't you change it?"

My mouth hung partially open as I rigorously racked my mind for a suitable answer.

His diaper was "heavy."

For those non-parents who don't know what a "heavy" diaper is, it ain't the weight of the cotton.

I thought about the reason that I hadn't changed it.

I left at 10:30 a.m. with them safely strapped down in car seat and seat belts. Though it's safer to put one in the middle, I had one on each side in the rear seat.

Why not the middle seat?

The two of them sitting together longer than five minutes next to each other without something separating them is just begging for trouble.

Two high-energy boys sitting next to each other...

"Owww!!! Josees threw that motorcycle at me," El (short for Nathaniel) hollered. I had forgotten not to leave any missiles nearby. I was taking El to T-ball practice. My wife always insists for some strange reason that I take Josees along.

I only had to tell them to behave four times during the 20-minute trip. They almost listened once.

I was busy diagramming in my mind a pop-up partition for the middle seat.

I have a 4-wheel Quadra Drive Jeep. It is powered by the largest V-8 Jeep makes. It will shift power to any wheel and is arguably the best stock off-road vehicle you can buy. The Jeep can handle steep hills and all types of rugged terrain.

That's on the outside. El and Josees in the back seat is an entirely different adventure that no amount of drive wheels or horsepower helps tame.

"Owww!" Josees exclaimed this time.
El had thrown the spare diaper at him. I pulled into the baseball center and parked in the first spot.

"Open my door first, open my door first," Josees demanded urgently. Neither likes to be outdone, even in such simple things as exiting the car.

It was about a quarter of a mile to the field where El played.

Kids walk at their own pace.
Each kid at a different pace.
They stop when they see something interesting.
They see something interesting every few feet.

There is a fork in the path leading to the baseball field.
One way goes to El's field, the other goes to the play gym
area.

It reminded me of decisions that we must often make,
two paths, two strong wills pulling in opposite directions.

El needed to go to the baseball field, Josees wanted to go
to the play gym area. Needs and wants often pull us in
different directions.

I picked Josees up and we all went to the baseball field.
In a few minutes Josees was sounding like an air raid
siren. He wanted to go to the play gym area.

I spent the two hours that El stayed on the field running
back and forth between the two areas, keeping an eye out
for one while trying to keep an eye on the other.

Josees made it through the slides of the play gym without
a scratch or bump. I gathered him up and went to El's
field as his practice ended. Josees jumped in the sandbox
near the field.

He fell. He hollered that his knee hurt and I carried him
back to the Jeep.

I took them to eat after that. I won't elaborate but eating
has it's own set of adventures.

Multiply the T-ball and sandbox by two and you get the picture.

I arrived home at 2:30 p.m. I opened Josees' door at the same time El opened his. They "tied" getting out.

I was a proud father.
I had gotten them back safely, back without a scratch except for the very small, barely visible indication of Josees' fall in the sandbox. I sure wasn't going to tell my wife about that. She would have thought I was negligent and wasn't watching him.

That wasn't true at all;
I was looking straight at him when he fell.

"Why didn't you change his diaper?"

Oh my goodness, I hadn't even thought about his diaper.

"What? Does it need changing?" was my response.

It sounded like an intelligent question to me.

"You've been gone four hours and you haven't changed his diaper!"

It was a MountainWings Moment.

No... not the type that's a flash of inspiration, but the type where you need to read MountainWings to get you over the hump.

We all do silly things that in the middle of the hustle and bustle don't seem silly at all.

We all forget.

We all look in retrospect and say,
"How could I have done that?"

We all have days with an extra load of un-removed heaviness.

As usual, the scratches are really minor when you look closely, and the heaviness easily removed with the right cleanser.

Next time, I'll make sure that I change his diaper,

provided that I can find it.

My Two Cents Worth
==================

I Love You!

"I Love You" is one of the shortest sentences in the English language.

It is also one of the most meaningful.

No matter how old we are, most people can still remember the first person they romantically loved.

There are many types of love:

Love for a sibling, parent, spouse, child, friend, object, pet or even a stranger.

We relate to so many people each and every day, but it is only during holidays that we stop and take time to show someone how much we really love them.

The most precious gift to my wife that I have ever given her cost me $0.02.

That was the cost of a piece of paper and some ink.

Even though not much money was spent on the poem I wrote for her, she knew much thought, love and caring went into writing it.

For those people in your life who mean something to you, take time out of your busy schedule today and just write a short note to them and tell them how much they mean to you.

Don't just hand it to them either, work those creative muscles and leave it somewhere they would not expect to find it.

I left my wife's taped next to the mirror where she sleeps with a sign saying "Here lies the most beautiful woman in the world" with an arrow pointing to her pillow.

Gifts of the heart won't cost you much money, but without them, you and the people you love will lose so much.

Go get your pen.

That's just my two cents worth.

A MountainWings Original by James Bronner

The Boss

=========

We were discussing life-changing statements.

You know, the type of statement that hits home so hard that it changes your thinking, forever steering you on a different path.

Some movies have that quality, some sermons, some people, some moments, and even some MountainWings. They literally drill their way into your spirit. You enter one person and exit another, forever influenced and changed by the encounter.

My mother and I were having dinner with a lawyer. It was not business but a friendly dinner with the lawyer, his wife, and two of their children.

He told a personal story about a life-changing statement and its effect that I feel will change the life course of at least one person who reads MountainWings.

This lawyer is the kind of man about whom I would say, "I want my son to turn out like him."

He is the kind of man that if I were forced to choose

another father I would say, "I would like a father like this man."

I have a great respect for this lawyer. He is the reason that I have never used a lawyer joke on MountainWings though lawyer jokes seem to be the most common kind on the net. His character is one of the best that I have seen among men, and each time I read a lawyer joke, I could never imagine him as that lawyer.

As I heard Attorney Bill Merritt speak, I knew that at least one MountainWings reader would be affected by what he said, possibly for life.

Maybe it's you.

Attorney Merritt began to tell the tale:
I had a professor in business school who like a marine drill sergeant constantly drilled one thing into us. I didn't think it was that significant at the time, but the drilling was so constant that when I graduated I automatically followed his advice (or drilling, whichever you want to call it). It's amazing what repetition will do.

We were all eager students, ready to conquer the world, ambitious, motivated, smart, loaded with dreams, and impatient to make our mark in the world.

The instructor's constant repetition was, "When you leave this school and look for a job, don't choose your job based on the salary. Don't choose your job based on the city. Don't choose your job based on the benefits or the prestige of the company.

Choose your first job on one criterion and one criterion only.

Choose it based on the character of your boss."

I thought that was a strange thing.
Not only strange but also difficult to determine.
I trusted my instructor and his voice wouldn't leave my head, so his advice ultimately guided my job search.

I ended up out in the middle of nowhere working for a diesel engine manufacturing company in the Midwest, Cummins Engine.

My boss was the CEO, Henry Schacht.
I didn't realize it until years after I started my own law firm that how I handled my business was exactly the way Schacht handled things.

I related to my secretary, to the other partners, to the paralegals, even to the clean-up crew in the exact way that Henry Schacht did. We called his quotes and ways "Shockisms."

I remember most vividly a meeting held by Schacht.
The CEO's of some major Fortune 500 companies were there. Most had flown in on private jets.

You've read about those types of jets. Multi-million dollar chariots with private bathrooms, couches, bars, large screen TV's, stereos, bedrooms, telephones, gourmet meals, you name it and they have it.

Most have never seen the inside of such luxury jets much

less flown in them. Those were the air cars these men flew in on.

There were eight or nine of some of the most powerful men in America around that table. Henry Schacht sat at the head.

I was awed and somewhat humbled being in the presence of such power, success, and wealth. These companies were blue chip all the way and here I was in the midst of them.

In the middle of the meeting, Schacht suddenly looked at his watch and said, "It's 4 o'clock, it's time for my son's soccer game," and he got up, excused himself and left.

I saw the jaws drop of every CEO at that table.

I could hear them thinking - "The nerve of this man to leave such an important meeting because his son has a soccer game. Doesn't he realize how many thousands of dollars per hour it costs just for my plane to fly me here? Doesn't he know how much my time is worth? All for a soccer game?"

Henry Schacht never missed a game that his son played.

Henry Schacht had his priorities in order.

I now understand the wisdom of my instructor. What seemed so silly at the time, as I look back at it, makes so much sense.

My first boss influenced me to a degree that I would have

never thought possible. I act so much like him that I now see why the instructor insisted that we choose our first full-time job based on the character of the boss.

That was Attorney Bill Merritt's story.

We were at his house because he wanted his children to meet my mother. My mother wanted his children to meet me. The point is, we were there because Attorney Merritt wanted his children to meet someone that he felt would add positive influence in their lives.

His children are doing great. Of the two present at the dinner, one had just graduated from Princeton and the other is a sophomore at Princeton, majoring in aerospace engineering.

Both had a peace and maturity of spirit that far exceeded youth of their age and most older adults.

Do you know what it felt like?

It felt like the children of a father who hadn't missed any soccer games, no matter what the cost.

The first boss's influence went beyond the boardroom.

For the student or person who has yet to enter their first career full-time job, this MountainWings may be for you. It's not something that you are generally taught, especially with the tight job market.

Maybe you don't need to think of leaving school and getting the first job that you can.

Maybe you need to think of school as making you really ready to learn and be shaped, like soft putty.

Maybe your first boss is the main sculptor.

Be careful whom you allow to shape you.

Henry Schacht is now chairman of Lucent Technologies.

I am willing to bet that he still has his priorities in order.

I am willing to bet that he still knows the true cost of a missed game and that it is too high of a price to pay.

Goodies

I had just finished my run and exited the shower.

My five-year-old son asked me, "Daddy, why do you run?"

"I run to stay healthy," I answered.

"Will running keep you healthy?" he inquired.

"Have you ever seen Daddy sick?" I asked him.

He pondered his memory and in his brief time on earth, he couldn't recall his father ever being sick.

"So running keeps you from getting sick?" he asked again.

"It helps but daddy does a lot of other things to stay healthy. Daddy eats healthy food and that helps too," I said figuring that would completely answer his questions.

"You don't eat any goodies?" he asked, pausing for my answer.

I paused.

"Goodies aren't good for you are they?"
he stated and waited.

"Not usually," I slowly answered.

"I only eat one goodie a day," he remarked.
"I know goodies aren't good for you, so that's why I only
eat one goodie a day," he said proudly.

I still paused.

Yes, I run.

Yes, I have an extremely healthy diet compared to the
standard.

Yes, I also have a "goodie" problem.

What are goodies?

My son never defined them and neither did I.
We both knew.

Goodies are not just things that taste good. Apples,
bananas, strawberries, oranges, watermelons, and the rest
of the fruits taste good, but they weren't what we were
talking about.

We were talking about goodies, the things that taste
good, but weren't particularly good for you. Usually,
goodies are not only not particularly good for you; they
are often particularly bad for you.

They taste good. Real good.

I have a particular weakness for Mr. Goodbars. I am a chemist by educational training. I understand more than most about the high amount of fat, sugar, salt, and other stuff in unhealthy excess in each bar. I understand the psychoactive effect of chocolate, read Weeds and Seeds on page 375.

With all of that understanding, that little yellow and red package often calls me from the shelf:

"Here I am!"
"I taste so good!"
"One or two of me won't hurt, you deserve it!"
"No one will know!"

You know the sound. The voice calling you may not be from a Mr. Goodbar, but you've got your own set of goodies. We all do.

Too often I have said, "no more goodies for me."

That held up fine until. . .

Until. . . I got weak
Until. . . The pressure of the week seemed to melt away in the brown world of a chocolate bar.

Goodies allow us a brief minute of escape.
On the day that my anti-goodie resolve breaks, I don't just eat one goodie, I eat far too many.

My son had a grasp of things.
He had set a limit.

One goodie a day.
I learned something from him that day,
"The law of the discipline of moderation."

I am NOT talking about the things that you should
absolutely stay away from, you know what those are too.
I am talking about the things in the "goodie" area.

I preached a sermon once about resisting temptation.
I told the congregation my greatest food temptation was
Mr. Goodbars because I liked them so much. A month
later, a member presented me with a box of 24 Mr.
Goodbars.

They remained unopened in my house for weeks.

Until. . .

Know anyone with a goodie problem?

Send this to them; my son has something to tell them.

Today I began cleaning some junk mail off my desk.

I was looking for some information that someone had faxed me.

I began shedding one letter after another off my desk. In the midst I found undeposited checks, unpaid bills, charity requests, a phone card, junk mail, and of course, the important information that I was originally looking for.

It reminded me so much of life.

The space on the desk represents time, the 24 hours of your day.

On it are things of varying value covering it completely.

The undeposited checks are the time that we should spend with the relationships in our life. Many checks expire if not cashed within a certain time. Over time without depositing time and attention into our relationships, our kids grow distant, our wives grow unloved, and our Creator remains unknown.

This is the most important time we have, but yet, many times the least used. We often judge its value simply by the paper it is printed on rather than by the amount of "funs" that will be deposited into our account.

The unpaid bills are the time that you spend at work. You need work to pay the bills, but if you by chance don't go to work, lights, water, phone, and heat will be cut off.

The charity requests represent the time we spend helping others.

The phone card that came represents time we spend just plain old talking on the phone.

The important information represents the time you spend finding your meaning in life, learning, and preparing for your destiny.

And then there was the "junk mail."

This is an area of life that often takes up the majority of the time of our day outside of work. If you work eight hours a day, take an hour lunch, spend one hour in traffic getting to and from work, sleep seven hours, eat and drink one hour, and get ready for work and bed one hour, you only have five hours left for the other things of life.

Of this remaining five hours, most dads spend five minutes or less of quality time with their children. The time that they spend listening to their wives, often they are thinking about other things that they would rather be doing.

The time we spend with God consists of saying the Lord's prayer before going to sleep.

Many even discard MountainWings as junk.

Most of the remaining five hours are spent on junk mail or junk e-mail; this is mail that makes no difference in your life if you throw it in the trash.

Watching T.V., gossiping, video games, reading material with no value, or even excess sleep would all fall into the junk mail category.

Of course life should contain a certain percentage of idle time just to give our minds relief, but let too much pile up and all too quickly you find yourself not able to find the important mail on the desk of life.

Where do you spend your time?

A MountainWings Original by James Bronner

I Made A 41

===========

Perhaps the only test score that I remember is the 41.
I was in high school. The class was taught by one of the
two teachers who impacted me most, Mr. Bales. The
other teacher was Mrs. Drew from the seventh grade.
It's amazing how I can remember from over 30 years ago
my two most impacting teachers.

The eighth grade. It was a time when I, like most, didn't
know what I was to be in life. The drama of that time of
youth was simply to get through school and make the
long walk home.

There are some things that will still be like the eighth
grade when you get to be eighty.

The test was the final for the class. I remember anxiously
waiting as Mr. Bales passed out test after test. It was a
rather difficult test. I didn't know how well I had done,
but I knew there were things on it that I didn't know.

The air whooshed around the pages as it made a gentle
sound plopping down. It was a rhythm as each student
received their test – plop, plop, plop.

I heard groan after groan that accompanied the plops.
I could tell by the groans that the grades weren't looking
good. Mr. Bales dropped the stapled pages on my desk.

There in big red numbers, circled to draw attention,
was my grade.
41...Groan!!!

I moved my paper where it wasn't in plain view, a 41 was not something that you wanted your classmates to see.

After the final plop, Mr. Bales stood behind the worn desk that had stood guard over countless students before me. He addressed the none too jubilant class.

"The grades were not very good, none of you passed, so I will have to consider grading on a scale," Mr. Bales announced.

"The highest grade in the class was a 41, so all of you flunked," were the final words that I remember.

A 41. That's me.

Suddenly my dismal looking final didn't look quite so bad. There were at least 30 students in the class. I had the highest grade. I felt a whole lot better.

I walked home that day with the low but high grade safely tucked away in my book satchel. My mother knew that I had a big test that day and asked me as soon as I got home, "How did you do on your test?"

"I made a 41," I said.

My mother's expression changed. A frown now stood where a smile was a few seconds earlier. I knew that I had to explain and explain fast. "But Mother, I had the highest grade in the class," I proudly stated.

I knew that statement would change things. I had the highest grade in the class, that made a difference.

My mother said, "You flunked."

"But I had the highest grade in the class!" I replied.

"I don't care what everyone else had, you flunked.
It doesn't matter if everyone else flunked too, what
matters is what you do," my mother firmly answered.

For years, I thought that was a harsh judgment.
My mother was always that way. It didn't matter what
the other kids did, it only mattered what I did and that I
did it excellently.

We often don't understand the wisdom of good parents
until we ourselves stand in the parenting shoes.
My mother's philosophy has carried me throughout life.
Don't worry about what the crowd does.
The crowd often goes the wrong way.

If you follow the crowd, you will go to the same destination as the crowd. The path of the crowd is wide and it
is crowded. The path to pass the tests of life is narrow
and there are very few people on it.

The path up the mountain is narrow; it is not crowded.
The path to health is narrow; it is not crowded.
The path to harmony, peace and happiness with your
spouse is narrow; it is not crowded.

The path to peace with yourself and the world is narrow;
it is not crowded.

I made a 41 and was proud of it, but it would not have
gotten me through the real tests.

The majority of spouses are not faithful, it's the crowd. Even though you may be the smoothest deceiver of the group, you are on the road to failure; it's not a passing grade.

The crowd eats fattening unhealthy fast food. That food sends you to an early appointment with the doctor and the funeral director. It's the food of the crowd.

The crowd spends no special time in prayer and meditation each day. That leads to an unhealthy spirit. It's the way of the crowd.

Thirty years after my mother said that she didn't care if I was the best failure in the class, I understand why.

"Wide is the gate and broad is the road that leads to destruction, and many enter through it. But small is the gate and narrow the road that leads to life, and only a few find it."

That's a quote that my mother lives by.

We often take comfort in the crowd; the only problem is that the crowd is not comfortable.

PASS the class!

30 Seconds
==========

In business I remember the flops, the failures, the plans that didn't work and the embarrassing moments as lessons of life.

My first speech was in fifth grade at a recital. The auditorium was full of parents and teachers. I was the only student whom the teacher did not have a copy of their speech.

Why?

Because I knew mine so well, the teacher hadn't bothered to keep a copy, she knew that I wouldn't mess up.

Halfway through the speech, my mind went blank.

Absolutely blank!

I remember looking at the audience, at the principal on the front row, at my parents. . .

I remember the teacher vainly trying to remember my next line and prompt me. For a full 30 seconds (although it seemed like 30 minutes) I just stood there.

Feeling naked. . .

I eventually remembered my next line and finished flawlessly.

I've never forgotten those 30 seconds in fifth grade.

I've never forgotten, but I've never gone blank in a speech since either. I've had instances where my speech was unavailable.

In one instance, I was the keynote speaker at a function. When I got to the podium the spotlights were so bright they cast a dark shadow over the podium and I couldn't read a word on the paper that contained my speech.

I continued on without the audience knowing anything was wrong.

I was keynote speaker at a banquet; when I got to the podium, I realized that I had left my speech under my chair.

I continued on without the audience knowing anything was wrong.

I was able to continue on because I remembered "30 seconds" in the fifth grade.
I remembered to not just stand there blank.

Do something, say something, but don't just stand there blank.

Both speeches turned out fine because of those embarrassing 30 seconds of feeling naked and what I learned from it.

t was one of the shortest, but toughest, lessons of my life.

No matter how embarrassing, how painful, how much the "I would rather be anywhere but here" feeling is, it is a lesson to be learned, whether it is 30 seconds, 30 minutes, or 30 years.

Learn the lesson well.

To Whom Much Is Given
=====================

A Mother was having a hard time getting her son to go to school in the morning.

"Nobody in school likes me," he complained.

"The teachers don't like me, the kids don't like me, the superintendent wants to transfer me, the bus drivers hate me, the school board wants me to drop out, and the custodians have it in for me. I just don't want to go to school."

"But, John, you have to go to school," said his mother sternly.

"You're healthy, you have a lot to learn, you have something to offer others, you are a leader.

And besides, you're 40 years old and
YOU ARE THE PRINCIPAL."

Have you ever felt like the principal in the above joke?

Mothers?
Bosses?
Husbands?
Even Pastors?

You are in charge; yet, the charges that you are in charge of can be a real challenge.

Leadership always has its price.
It's full of rewards, but the price can be heavy.

Everyone expects you to boost them, but who boosts you?

I was in the church one day.
I was alone (at least no other person was there).

The day had been hectic and the responsibilities great.
I stood in the sanctuary and asked God,
"Why do I have to do so much?"

I had the burdens of the church, the burdens of two businesses, and a family to deal with. Plus, I had my own stuff. Everyone has their own stuff in addition to other's stuff. Your own stuff hides in the corners of your mind just waiting for an opportunity to jump forth.

Your own stuff is enough to deal with by itself.

Do you remember seeing the pictures of Atlas? He is the Greek titan with the world on his shoulders. That's what it feels like sometimes. I'm sure you know the feeling.

I stood as the echoes of my voice slowly faded.
"Why did I have to do so much?"

I clearly heard God breathe a soft answer into my spirit, but it wasn't complete. It was half of a sentence and half of a statement.

"to whom much is given. . ."

hat was my answer, "to whom much is given. . ."

here is a quote that goes "you can judge a man by
hether he will ask for a light load or a strong back."

's the principle of the principal.

o whom much is given. . . much is required."

. MountainWings Original (except for the principal joke)

Pritty Good
===========

This is an actual MountainWings submission,
it is unedited.

submission= I was born with Cerebral Palsy. When I was
told of my disabillity, they tokd my parents to put me
away in a institution, because i would never be able to do
any thing for m yself. well here it is 36 years later, and I
have my own car, appartment, job. I drive that car without hand controlls, I have it pritty good thanks to My
Lord Jesus Christ.

This fellow (name withheld) has it pretty good.

He really does.

Life is not what it is, it's what you think it is.
So, what do you think it is?

Life is not about what you have, it's about what you
appreciate.
So, what do you appreciate?

Life is not about what you are born with,
It's about what you do with what you have.
So, what are you doing with what you have?

Life is not about how well you spell or how eloquent you
speak; it's about what you are really saying.
Life is. . .
This fellow has it pritty good. Do you?

Better Than A Rolls
= = = = = = = = = = = = = = = = =

I spent four hours one night cleaning my wife's van. It was spotless and fragranced with powdered honeysuckle. That's what the car fragrance smelled like that I used.

As we were driving away the next day for a family outing, I looked in the back seat. The four-year-old was strapped in. The two-year-old was comfortably seated in his child seat. My wife was driving.

It was a MountainWings Moment.

MountainWings Moments occur whenever life gives us the opportunity to take an otherwise mundane or even negative situation and rise to the mountaintop.

I inhaled deeply the soft honeysuckle. It was mixed with the scent of the hair conditioner of the two-year-old. The kids were watching a video.

I was openly pleased with the cleaning job that I had done.

Every scrap, smudge, and drop of unidentifiable kid's stuff was gone.

"This van is great," I said.
"It's not a Rolls," my wife replied.

"No," I answered, "It's better than a Rolls Royce."

"A Rolls doesn't ride this smooth."

I have learned to find and appreciate MountainWings Moments.

We have a four-year-old Plymouth Voyager Van.
I have ridden in a Rolls Royce; it wasn't a new Rolls, but I wasn't impressed for the money.

A Rolls doesn't have the headroom of the van.
A Rolls doesn't have a TV.
A Rolls doesn't have a VCR.
A Rolls can't seat seven people or let you listen to three sound systems at one time.
In a Rolls you can't recline the seat into a bed.

I went down the list of all of the advantages of our van over a Rolls.

"You have a point," my wife said.

So often, the thing that you have is so much better than what is on the other side of the fence.

You just don't realize it.

You have to get on the mountain to see it.

You need A MountainWings Moment.

A strange thing happened after that day.

Neatness of organization is not my wife's strength.

The van is usually piled with her papers, kid's toys, and all of the accessories that go along with kids.

I got in the van a week later.

I was shocked. It was absolutely clean.

Two weeks later.

Still spotlessly clean.

I rode with my wife yesterday (a month later), I had a fruit bar with me. I unwrapped it and laid the wrapper on the spotless floor behind me.

"Don't leave that wrapper on the floor," she said as she eyed the wrapper with an extreme look of disdain.

A month ago, you would not have been able to find the wrapper if you laid it on the floor, and the van would have qualified as Oscar's vehicle on "The Odd Couple" (he was the junky one).

Today, it was like Felix's (the neat one).

What in the world happened?

I was both proud and amazed.

I asked, "What caused the change from junk mobile to showroom condition?"

"If I wouldn't junk up a Rolls, then why should I junk up something better than a Rolls?"

Same Van – Different Appreciation

How we treat something depends so much on how we view and value it.

When you stop to think about it, you have a lot of things in your world far more valuable than a Rolls Royce. The eyes you use for reading this are two of those many things.

Maybe there are some people and some things that you need to put polish on, lavish sweet smelling things on, and remove the junk from.

Maybe, just maybe, you're junking up something better than a Rolls Royce.

Itty Bitty Things
===============

Several months ago, the unsubscribe command on MountainWings was not working for a brief period.

We received an e-mail from a lady who said she had tried to unsubscribe, but she was still receiving issues. I didn't see how that could be possible, so I unsubscribed her and then checked the database. Her e-mail address was still there.

I finally tracked down what was wrong. An itty-bitty character was missing from the unsubscribe script. I don't know how it disappeared, it just disappeared.

Computers are a lot like life.

An itty-bitty thing can stop or start the whole process.

Both the male sperm and the female egg are so small that no human eyesight can see them. They are itty-bitty things.

The beginnings of most things, good or bad, are itty-bitty things. Even MountainWings began from an itty-bitty thing.

Most affairs or marriages begin with an itty-bitty thing. A sideward glance held a fraction of a second longer than necessary.

A casual brush of clothing.
A hello with a bit more bounce per ounce.
A smile.

Itty-Bitty things.

When you find out the true story, you discover that most divorces begin with itty-bitty things.

What kids will remember most about their early childhood will be an itty-bitty thing to an adult.

Maybe there was one person who needed a particular issue of MountainWings during that period. They would not have received it except for that itty-bitty thing.

If that's you, e-mail us and let us know.

For those of you who did unsubscribe and are still getting issues, it's working now. The itty-bitty thing has been fixed and the unsubscribe is working perfectly. Maybe it was working perfectly all along.

Perfection just may not be what we think.
Itty-Bitty things lead to Great Big things.
There is nothing insignificant.

The Second Hill
===============

Are you running that hill or is that hill running you?

That's a question a man asked me today as I was jogging.

He was standing by his car, I was breathing hard as I moved up the hill where he was parked. His question plagued me.

Each day presents us with hills.

Hills, bills, chills, spills, thrills, deals, kills, pills, wills, and nils...

We have them all sooner or later.

Are they running you or are you running them?

Each hill or uphill climb in our lives tries to tire us, make us quit, or at the very least, make us complain.

You can't avoid getting tired.

I don't care how much exertion your physical or mental conditioning can withstand, a steep enough hill will make you tired.

Whether the hill is running you doesn't depend upon whether you are tired. There are those who are tired even though they are sitting in rocking chairs.

The hill runs you when it gets you down. I refuse to let that happen. I know the hills make me stronger, that's why I run them. Every hill in my life has made me stronger.

If you run your hills instead of them running you, they will make you stronger too.

You'll be in better shape.

You'll get tired, but eventually the same hill will get easier and easier.

One day, even the hills will be no challenge.

You'll seek a mountain.

Don't worry, you've got Wings.

The Trickle

==========

My Jeep battery was dead this morning.

I had just returned from a weeklong trip.

The Jeep is only six months old. The battery is big and new.

I hadn't left any lights on.

What happened with the Jeep happens to many of us.

I had three power adapters plugged into the cigarette lighter sockets. I had installed a triple cigarette lighter socket. I don't smoke, but I have a lot of gadgets that need plugging up. I have three cell phones. What in the world do I need with three cell phones? That's another story. None of the phones were plugged up, only the three power adapters were plugged up, and their little LED lights were glowing.

Even though they have very low power drains, these three little lights completely drained a big, powerful, and new battery.

That illustrated a very important life lesson.

Constant withdrawals without deposits will eventually run your account dry.

No matter how small the withdrawal, sooner or later, your account will run dry.

That's what happens with most marriages.

Little by little, day by day, small withdrawals are made from the love bank.

A slight criticism here, a minor remark there, a compliment opportunity missed, and the love bank in a few years is dry.

The relationship won't start.

In all things, make sure that you add more than you take. No matter how small, let the trickle be positive.

When you do that, not only will your own battery never run dry, you'll have enough power left over to boost someone else off.

The Rear View Mirror
===================

When driving along the interstate during rush hour, most of us keep our eyes on the road and what's ahead of us.

Rarely do we ever keep our eyes on what's behind us and what's to the left or right of us for more than a few seconds at a time.

Yet, concerning many matters in our lives, we fail to look ahead and keep driving along.

When faced with some tough and trying times in life, we tend to look around and look behind instead of looking ahead.

We often allow mistakes to resurface. That's driving by looking into the rear view mirror. By wondering 'what if' won't change the past.

Again, we're taking our eyes off of the road ahead.

Once you know where you are going and who you are, you'll begin to focus on what's ahead of you more often.

There is nothing wrong with remembering the past mistakes, heartaches, trials, and tribulations.

There is something wrong with living in the past.

You have to keep the faith and stop looking behind you and to the left or right. You're never going to get ahead by looking back. If you do, you're liable to have a wreck.

It's time to move forward!

by Britte Blair, Assistant to Nathaniel Bronner

Half

= = = = =

Half of the mistakes made in your relationship will most likely be yours.

That's a deep but mathematically accurate thought.

It is typical in our church men's meeting to talk about all of the things that women do in the relationships.

From what I've heard, the women's meeting is the same.

All of the quirks, the errors, the unappreciative and inconsiderate things, how "they" have to be babied, if only "they" were more mature, and that it is a good thing that "we" are so much more mature in order to be able to put up with "them."

Yet in truth, each side makes about half of the mistakes.

It is always difficult to see our own faults.
It's always easy to see the other person's shortcomings.

I sometimes wonder "where has the love gone?"

You rarely hear anyone say, "I know they've got their weaknesses, but I love them so much that it doesn't matter."

You rarely hear anyone say, "I got in this for better or for worse, in sickness and in health, rich or poor, that's what I said and that's what I mean, and I'm so glad I married him/her."

We had one man in the men's meeting recently; he had been married for 46 years and said that he loved his wife a thousand times more now than he did when he married.

He was the oldest man in the group.

He was also perhaps the wisest.

It was refreshing.

You hear so much of the things wrong in relationships, but you very rarely hear how much in love a couple is.

Even if people feel it, they don't say it very much.

Neither of them.

Now who's fault is that?

Half The Wave
===============

I am writing to tell you how very much I enjoy receiving your writings in my mailbox every day.

I look forward to reading each and every one. I have a folder that I keep them all in. You have made me think a lot about my life and my family.

The MountainWings issue "HALF" that you sent out was one that everybody should read!

I also wanted to tell you a little story that happened to my family and me last year. Sorry if it is a little long, but I feel it is worth sharing.

A year ago, my husband and I were having a lot of problems in our lives. We didn't want to see that our problems were not all one-sided, that it was HALF of his and HALF mine. So we split up and got a divorce.

We were only separated for three months and neither of us could stop thinking about the other, even though we tried to go on with our lives with other people. We just kept getting in touch with each other, until finally, we went two weeks without speaking.

I was staying with a good friend of mine. She watched my daughter for me one day so that I could take a walk and have some time for my thoughts because "The Waves" of life were drowning me.

As I was out walking, I asked God what He wanted from me and for Him just to tell me, and I would try and do whatever it was that He had planned for me. I am sure that people driving past must have thought I was a little crazy walking down the street looking at the sky talking to myself.

I guess God knew what He wanted for me.

About that time, my ex-husband pulled up and offered me a ride. Now this is on a street that we hardly ever went down.

At first, I refused the ride and he left. My ex-husband drove past about four more times; finally the last time, he told me that there was no sense in putting blisters on my feet, he would take me wherever I was going.

To shorten the story, I took the ride and we talked.

A week later, we started planning our wedding!

We got remarried, and we have never been happier!!!!

Everyday I thank God for not giving up on us and for not letting us give up on the most precious gifts: love, happiness and knowing you are with the one whom God had intended you to love for all time.

My submarine to face all the waves of the world with!

Heather from Florida

One Nice Person

=================

I was headed to Cincinnati Ohio.

The plane was due to leave at 5 p.m. I was to connect to a flight from Charlotte, NC at 7:10, and from Charlotte fly to Cincinnati.

It was raining. The flight was late. It was very late.

By 6:45, the gate attendant asked for all passengers with connections in Charlotte before 7:45 to come to the counter.

The line was long, very long, and very slow moving.

At 7:00 the plane took off. There were still people in the line who had connecting flights in Charlotte before 7:45.

I was one of those in the line.

It was obvious that we weren't going to make the connecting flight. There was only one gate agent handling the connecting passengers. He furiously worked finding alternatives on other airlines. Sometimes there were none.

Passengers were upset and they made it known.

The man beside me was from London. There were no available flights anywhere that would get him to London on time. He would be at least a day late.

"I work with the public," he said.

He explained, "The public often doesn't understand what a person behind the counter has to go through. It's not their fault. They didn't cause the rain or the mechanical problems or set the policies.

Yet they have to bear the brunt of the cursing, the fussing, the anger and the frustration that the public releases. It can be a real tough job. But you know one nice person can change your whole day. Just one nice person out of the angry mob can really make a difference."

It was a MountainWings Moment.

I looked around.

Everyone (at least most everyone) was angry and frustrated.

I could hear the elevated voices and the complaining as the agent patiently tried to explain that was all that he could do.

Was there one nice person in the crowd?

One nice person who would ease the burden on the agent's shoulders.

One nice person who could "make his day."

The next time you are in such a situation, look around for the one nice person.

If you don't see them, then you have a chance to make someone's day. You have a chance to ease the pain.

You have a chance to become the light in the midst of darkness.

Suppose you don't. Suppose you fuss and vent along with the rest of them. You won't get to your destination one bit faster.

Suppose you become the one nice person. You won't get to your destination one bit faster either. But you will have made one person's journey much more pleasant.

Maybe your decision won't change your destination but it might change where you are heading.

Because there are some places where only nice people are allowed.

GPS

====

I am a gadget man.

I don't have much in terms of jewelry, virtually none in fact. I don't have a fancy house or wear fancy clothes (except Sunday). I do have a lot of gadgets.

I bought a new GPS unit. A GPS unit is a Global Positioning System receiver. The GPS system was developed by the military to guide missiles to their targets and other military things.

It's the system that allows you to determine exactly where you are anywhere on earth. GPS allows cars with built-in navigation systems to direct you to where you are going.

This unit, a Garmin GPSV, sits on the dash of the car. I loaded the detailed map of Atlanta and was ready for the unit to tell me how to get anywhere in the city that I wanted to go.

I tested it with places where I knew where I was going. It directed me there perfectly, telling me in advance which way to turn and how far I had to go before the next turn.

My confidence grew in the GPSV and its ability to lead me where I wanted to go. A couple of things that the manual didn't tell me were quickly answered by tech support and I was now navigating with ease.

This makes it easy as I travel. I can download the map of the city that I am going to before I leave. When I get there and rent a car, I just put the unit on the dash, program where I am going and let it tell me how to get there.

Today, my wife asked me to drive her to the doctor. She is 7 months pregnant and wanted me to drive her. I told her OK.

The appointment was at 10 a.m. and she asked me to come home by 9:15. I had an early morning meeting and left the meeting in order to arrive home in ample time.

The doctor had moved since my wife last saw him. She had a general idea where to go and had even printed out computer directions from a mapping service on the Internet.

I entered the address into the GPSV and punched "GoTo."

"Are you sure that thing works?" my wife asked.

"Yes, I'm sure it will take us straight there," I replied.

"My computer directions say we will get there in 30 minutes and I don't want to be late," my wife commented. It was 9:25 as we were leaving. The computer directions would have us there by 9:55 if there were no traffic snarls.

"This will get us there Puddin," I said as we drove away and the GPSV locked on the satellites.

We got to the expressway, the GPSV said to go West, Puddin's computer sheet said to go East.

Puddin raised a concerned eyebrow as I headed West; the arrow on the GPSV was steadily pointing West. It took us to a back road. Puddin sat up with a furrowed brow.

"I've never been this way before! This doesn't look right! I am going to be late!" she exclaimed.

I hadn't been that way before either. The path did look unfamiliar and somewhat suspect.

The GPSV twisted and turned as it took us through a labyrinth of roads. Puddin got increasingly anxious.

"Didn't you want me to drive you?" I asked. "Yes, but it looks like that thing doesn't know where it's going, and I think we are going in circles," she said.

"Sit back and relax, not only will you get there, but you will get there early. This is a lesson in life. It is a little thing. Worry won't help. You don't have to drive, just relax, I will get you there," I said.

Puddin was sitting straight up. She and a 7-month-old baby in the womb were on edge. I stopped the Jeep.

"Lean the seat back and relax," I said.

"I don't want to lean back, I don't want to relax, and we are going to be late."

"If you don't lean the seat back, I will pull the Jeep into that parking lot and not move until you lean back and relax," I insisted.

Reluctantly, under the threat of not moving at all, Puddin leaned the seat back.

"Now close your eyes."

"I don't want to close my eyes."

"Eyes closed or parking lot," I said.

We pulled into the parking lot of the doctor's building at 9:42 a.m., 13 minutes ahead and almost twice as fast as the computer's directions. The little GPSV accurately led us the shortest and fastest way to our destination.

We need to rely more on GPS.

Not the Global Positioning System,
but the God Positioning System.

We don't know all of the roads. We don't know the shortest route. We can't see an overview of all of the territory.

If we just learn to depend upon the right kind of GPS, follow the directions, and relax along the way, it would make all of our journeys a lot smoother.

I am sitting here in the doctor's office now typing this issue on my laptop. The doctor has not come into the examination room yet. It's 10:55, almost an hour later.

Puddin is getting antsy again.

I can almost hear God telling some of you now:

"Sit back and relax, not only will you get there, but you will get there early. This is a lesson in life. It is a little thing. Worry won't help. You don't have to drive, just relax, I will get you there. If you don't learn to relax and trust Me, I will pull over and leave you parked until you have faith enough."

You are not going in circles, though you often think that you are. You will get there, though it may not be in the timing that you choose. You do need to close your eyes and relax while the right GPS system works.

As the doctor's lateness passes the 1-hour mark, I tell Puddin again as I tell you. . .

"This is a lesson in life.

Sit back, close your eyes, and relax."

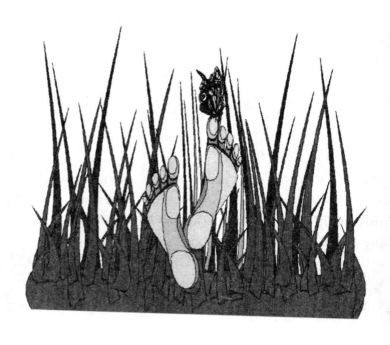

The Barefoot Golfer

=================

After the first hole, he always removed his shoes. He owned the finest golf shoes but preferred grass to leather.

He was the barefoot golfer.

He was my father.

If you are not familiar with golf, it is played in shoes with cleats, metal or plastic spikes that help keep your feet firmly planted. My father wouldn't wear golf shoes. As soon as he played the first hole and was out of sight of the clubhouse, he removed his fancy shoes. The golf course had an unspoken "no shoes, no service" policy.

Why did my father play golf without shoes?

It began with something that he read. I don't know where he read it, his room was a jumble of books on every subject that could improve life. He said that every organ in the body has nerve endings that terminate in the feet. When you walk on the ground, especially if dew is still on it, it creates a very small electrical current that energizes and helps the whole body.

My father in his '70s would walk each morning in the wet grass right after he finished standing on his head for 30 minutes.

Yes, he was a very unusual man.

He was by average terms a wealthy man. He had built a very successful business. He had six sons (four became ministers) and a wife whom he had been married to for nearly 40 years.

He was one of the most highly respected businessmen in the city.

Yet, he played golf in bare feet.

He understood some things about being grounded that you would do well to learn. Shoes won't do it. Yes, they help to firm up your stance and theoretically should help your golf game, but shoes don't make the difference in the real game of life.

My father was a physically small man. He stood about 5' 7" tall. He moved the scale to only 145 pounds. He had an extremely outgoing personality and could befriend anyone anywhere. He found golf partners no matter where he traveled.

He didn't even have a fancy golf bag or a full set of clubs. He carried only the bare essentials. He would team up with strangers and join their group. They would eye him as someone who would probably slow them down and diminish from the challenge and fun of the game.

On the second hole when they saw him remove his shoes, they would glance at each other and wonder, "what kind of country player is this?" His swing wasn't even standard. My father's right shoulder was higher than his left. It came from many years of delivering newspapers in his youth with the heavy bag of papers slung over his shoulder. He compensated for his shoulders with an awkward looking swing.

The other players thought at least he'd be fun with his wit and smile if not a challenge.

The thing is, 95% of the time, he won.

By the time they got to the last hole, they knew that this little man in bare feet was something to reckon with.

My father taught me that more often than not, the best way would be different from the way of the crowd. Learn truth my son, and learn to walk in it," was his constant message to me.

That same message is constantly imbedded in MountainWings.

Has life's burdens and circumstances made one of your shoulders higher than the other?

You can still win, even with a handicap, you just may need to swing differently.

So what if you don't have the fancy stuff?
You can still win.

So what if you don't even have any golf shoes?
You can still win.

Tensed up and stressed out?

Take a bit of advice from my father, the barefoot golfer.

Get up early in the morning while the grass is still wet. Take off your shoes and spend ten minutes walking in the grass.

It's free. If you don't feel better - then what have you lost?

I recently bought a set of golf clubs to begin playing again.

I also bought a fancy pair of golf shoes.

I will wear those fancy shoes when I play,

on the first hole.

The Third Level

================

Today, I will illustrate third level thinking.

Many of you have already traveled to the third level.

I recently sent an e-mail requesting that all who intended to unsubscribe from MountainWings because they didn't like it or it wasn't benefiting them to do so now, so that we wouldn't move into a new rate structure for the month's e-mailing.

That e-mail was really multi-purposed. Yes, it is true that we are close to the current limit. I mainly realized that many on the MountainWings list did not sign up themselves. A friend or relative signed them up.

We don't have what's called a double opt-in system. That's a system where you must respond from your e-mail address before you will be added to the mailing list. Double opt-in prevents anyone from signing you up without your permission.

Some were signed up on MountainWings without their permission. For those who were and didn't like MountainWings, I wanted to make sure that we didn't intrude upon anyone. The e-mail limit gave anyone who didn't really want to receive MountainWings but may have felt obligated to a friend or relative, an easy way out.

On the first of next month, we will triple our e-mail capacity. We will then have the opposite situation. We will have an excess capacity. I won't like to see that excess capacity go to waste, but I don't want to impose on one single person.

So what's third level thinking?

The three levels are:

1. Thought
2. Words
3. Action

I will use MountainWings to illustrate this.

Those of you who stayed, 97%, obviously think well of MountainWings. Even many who unsubscribed wrote and said they had multiple e-mail addresses and was having MountainWings sent to all of them and were unsubscribing the extra ones.

For the 97% who stayed, all think positive thoughts about MountainWings. That's the first level, the level of thought.

The second level is the level of words.

Many e-mailed (words), about how MountainWings was blessing them and some were even afraid that it was being discontinued.

No, it is here to stay and there will never be a monetary charge for MountainWings.

Words are powerful.

Think of how many times you have been down and a cheerful or encouraging word from a stranger has helped you make it through the day and added sunshine.

On the opposite note, think how a caustic remark or an untactful criticism has kept you up at night, unable to sleep.

Words are powerful; they are the second level.

Many e-mailed and said they would like to make a contribution to MountainWings. Some said they would even pay $30.00 a year to subscribe to MountainWings. You asked in droves how you could financially contribute.

That's the third level. Action!

I will tell you how you can contribute.

Whatever amount you wanted to financially contribute to MountainWings, take that amount and help a stranger with it.

MountainWings is in no danger of being discontinued.

Third-level thinking automatically encompasses the first two levels and greatly surpasses them.

Take your job as an example.

Everyone knows of someone at the job who is having problems. It doesn't even need to be someone who is having problems, just someone who's maybe helped you or that you admire.

Suppose you went to them and said, "I really admire the way that you (fill in the blank), it really influenced me and helped to make me better. I would really appreciate it if you would accept this $5.00 and let me help buy your lunch today."

Thought, words, action – The Third Level.

If it's a male-female relationship, make sure there are no romantic undercurrents; this is about helping someone, not getting a date.

That little $5 would make a major impact in someone's life.

It could very well be the best lunch that they have had in years. It may even be a lunch seasoned with tears as they think there is at least someone who appreciates them.

Everyone has the power for third level living. Some may think, "I don't have any money to spare." It doesn't have to be money, that's just one example. And you do have money to spare.

Just skip your lunch to buy someone else's. It won't hurt you, it will actually do you good, I should know. I wrote the book on it, http://www.quickfasting.com.

MountainWings is limited. There is just so much that MountainWings can do, but those who read it have 100,000 times more potential for good. The ultimate purpose of MountainWings is not just to make you feel good but to take you to the level where you make others feel good.

Things of true power and good have within them the seeds of reproduction.

The third level is not some strange philosophy, so don't look for it in some mystic book. It is a simple principle that is practiced by anyone who makes the world better.

It's the simple principle of thinking a good thought, saying a good thing, and then, no matter how small, doing something good for someone.

I saw by the outpouring of support for MountainWings that many of you have moved to the third level.

Each of you has someone whom you see every day who needs your help. Maybe it's your boss and he doesn't need your $5.00.

No, maybe he doesn't need your $5, but I can guarantee that your boss needs the thought of you having enough admiration to part with your $5.00.

I know you need help too but that's not the point. You have the power to help another with something as simple and inexpensive as lunch and a few words of praise.

It may not only be the best lunch that they've had in years; it may also be the best lunch that you've missed in years.

Remember mountaintops are never crowded.
Few live on the third level. You can.
You bless others immensely when you travel there.
One small step at a time.
Maybe that first step will begin at lunchtime.

The Third Level

The Lowest Low
= = = = = = = = = = = = = =

Dear Friends,

I just read today's e-mail "You will meet them too" and it helped me very much.
Thank you.

Last Saturday, our daughter, 17 years old, told us that her grandfather (my father-in-law) had been molesting her for the past four months. At the beginning only with dirty talk, but Saturday morning he touched her. We are talking about an educated, rich, and important person.

You can imagine my feelings.

You can imagine what thoughts crossed my mind. There is no way I'd go for the 2nd or 3rd choice from today's e-mail, but it helped me not to feel that anger and all the feelings in the first choice that will hurt me, my wife and my daughter.

Please write me something, we are having a very tough time.

Thank you again

There are a few MountainWings requests that warrant an immediate answer and an answer that many may benefit from.

This is one of them.

Although I answered him long ago, I reprint my answer now for the benefit of all.

It is difficult to understand the depth of emotion that a parent experiences when something like this happens. It's not just the child, it's the other adult who is a close and trusted member of the family.

If someone were to molest one of my little boys, it would be very difficult for me not to do that person serious physical harm. That's the truth of it. This is the type of thing that calls everything that you profess to the carpet.

It can put your spirit in a place that I call, The Lowest Low.

These things can tear a family and individuals apart.
They can scar a child for life.
They are the creatures and the monsters that lurk in the darkest and deepest part of the valley.
They are real.

First, there is no excuse for what your father-in-law did.

None. Although there is no excuse, it helps to at least understand.

Most sexual attacks and molestations occur among people who know each other. It most likely won't be by a stranger in a dark alley. It is most often by a person with the same bloodline flowing in their veins as the victim.

Relatives.

Education, income, or social status won't diminish the possibility. The only thing that greatly diminishes the probability is sex. Women don't do such things as a general rule. It will by far most likely be a man.

I am a Pastor of a Christian church. My reference point is the Bible. For those of you who don't believe in it or know it, permit me the luxury of using what I know to illustrate a point.

Most of you will be familiar with the major characters in the Bible. Let's just take the wisest and most educated, the wealthiest, the bravest, and the strongest men in the Bible.

These are all Old Testament characters where much of their life is detailed.

Samson was the strongest man. He killed 1,000 men with the jawbone of an ass, a massive feat by any standards. The strongest man today would do amazingly well to handle ten men much less 1,000.

His parents warned Samson. Samson was even shown by the continual deceptiveness of the woman, Delilah, that she was not good for him. Still, Samson lost his strength and honor because he could not resist a forbidden woman.

David was the bravest. He killed Goliath with only a slingshot. David slept with another man's wife and then committed murder to cover up his adultery. He brought a curse upon himself and his family because he did not resist a forbidden woman.

Solomon was the wisest and perhaps wealthiest man in the Bible. He understood the vast things of science and the world and dazzled scholars from around the world with his brilliance.

He had 700 wives and 300 concubines. Solomon was told by God not to be involved with women of different religions. He, like his father, fell to forbidden women.

The wisest, wealthiest, bravest, and strongest, all fell to their lust for forbidden women.

So did your father-in-law.

These things usually don't just happen. They evolve. It begins in the mind with a casual thought that slowly begins to occupy more and more of his time.

The thoughts become words, on the edge at first, then more daring.

The words eventually become a touch.

Your situation is a delicate one. Not only is he your father-in-law, but your wife's father, and your daughter's grandfather.

He has not lost the right to be loved by you and your family.

He has lost the right to ever be alone with any children or to be completely trusted in that area again.

That needs to be made absolutely clear, no exceptions.

You still have the three choices:

1. Fight
2. Forget
3. Forgive and pray for them

Those three choices STILL will affect you the greatest.

When Jesus said, "Love your enemy," there was not a degree of enemy placed on the definition of enemy.

Did the definition of enemy stop at slanderous words that hurt your feelings or a sharp sword trying to cut your head off?

There was no limit placed on the enemy, just as there was no limit placed on the love.

I cannot advise you on the legal steps to take, that is your choice. I can advise you on the matters of your heart, that also, is your choice.

Forgive him, love him, but never leave him alone with your children again.

You will have to make such a choice again, maybe not

with your father-in-law but there will be others and other things that will send you back to the same three choices.

I hope you make the right decision.

Because of the delicate nature of this, I asked Dr. Shorter to also give an answer. Dr. Shorter attends our church and answers many of the Advice Requests on MountainWings.

from Dr. Shorter:
Praise your daughter for having the courage to tell.

It is extremely difficult for a child to disclose molestation when the abuser is a relative, there are added fears and complications. The child often knows instinctively that by disclosing she will be putting the parents in a position of having to choose between their child or the abuser.

Parents usually go into denial. Parents and society have a high tendency to dismiss the seriousness of the offense when it involves a close family member. You must handle this situation carefully.

The fallout of this type of abuse for your daughter could be:
Unhealthy relationships with men;
A sense of worthlessness;
Low self-esteem;

Unfounded guilt.

Parents, believe her. These claims are almost never made up. Affirm her.

Let her know she did the right thing by telling.
Remind her that she's not to blame.

Don't bring up forgiveness right now.
For most victims of molestation, forgiving the abuser can
only happen at the end of the healing process, not at the
beginning.

Forgive and forget is translated into deny and ignore.
Reunification must be handled slowly and carefully.

You cannot fix this problem and you cannot ignore it.
If you don't address it with the abuser, he will do it
again. You must decide whether you are going to be part
of the problem (by ignoring what the grandfather did) or
part of the solution (confronting the grandfather and perhaps reporting him to the authorities).

A child abuser needs help.
If you cover this up, you risk encouraging this act again.

There is a Christian Counselor Trained in this area. Give
them a call and get some step-by-step advice.
1-800-NEWLIFE. This is very serious and you must
consider the mental well being of your daughter.

Dr. Shorter

Deaf Coffee
=============

If you yelled for 8 years,
7 months and 6 days,

you would have produced
enough sound energy to
heat one cup of coffee.

The next time you feel like a yelling frenzy,
think about that.

Much of the energy in yelling is wasted.

Coffee doesn't hear you.

People do.

And it only takes one second of yelling

...to heat them up.

Coffee anyone?

A Pain-Free Day
= = = = = = = = = = = = =

A prayer request wished
that the sun would shine
warm on our face and
that we would have a
pain-free day.

It made me more thankful for today.

I don't have any pain.

You don't think about it until you've got a toothache.
You don't think about it until you've got a headache.
You don't think about it until you've got something else
aching on your body.

A pain-free day is a real luxury if you've got pain,
physical or otherwise.

I'm thankful as I sit here and type this.

I don't have carpel tunnel syndrome.
My fingers and wrist feel fine.
My eyes don't hurt.
I don't have hemorrhoids as I sit and my feet feel fine.

A pain-free day.

What a blessing.

You Are Beautiful!

=================

You are beautiful. . .

It's a phrase that my mother uses a lot.

I used to wonder, "How in the world can Mother call them beautiful?"

I am a logical, statistical man.
I call things as I see them.
I didn't see beauty.

My mother would tell people this with an enthusiasm they could feel. She was genuine. She wasn't telling them they were beautiful to get something from them. Most of the time, they were trying to get something from her.

I wondered for years what was wrong with Mother's perception and vision.

Couldn't she see that all of the people she called beautiful, weren't beautiful?

You were beautiful only if you had a certain figure and face that was classed as beautiful by the laws of the world and glamour. Yet when my mother spoke, people smiled as though Glamour magazine had listed them as one of the beautiful people of the year.

It took me years to finally understand my mother's vision and the phrase, "Beauty is in the eye of the beholder."

My mother had a spirit that could see the beauty in a person.

Most only look on the outside and then compare what they see with the standards the world has given them.

That was what I was doing.

Today when you leave your house, carefully look at the first person whom you see and notice how beautiful they are.

They may be balding, fat, wrinkled, pimply, or any of the other things the world frowns upon as beauty.

Look at them closely and look for the beauty.

If you really look, you'll see it.

I didn't believe that at first until I tried it. Sure enough, as I stared and opened another set of eyes, I was able to see the beauty in every person. No matter how rough or worn a person looked, each pain etched line held a glimpse of beauty.

You just had to look for the beauty.

It's there.

When you leave your home this morning, look hard at each person. You will start to see the beauty of every human who you didn't know existed.

Trust me and try this.
If you sincerely look, you will see it.

When you get home after seeing the beauty in faces you see, look in the mirror.

You are beautiful.

Thank you mama for all of the beauty that you have not only seen but added.

The Stairs

=============

This morning I stood at the top of the stairs to our basement and watched my two-year-old son journey down the stairs.

He was on his way to catch his mother. He was afraid his mother would leave without him and head for his school.

I desperately wanted to take him by the hand and walk him down the stairs. But I knew that if I never let him do it on his own, he would always depend on the balancing power of his father's hand.

Instead, I simply stayed close behind ready to move in an instant if he appeared to fall.

With his little legs and fragile sense of balance, he could not just walk down the stairs like an adult could. He sat down on his bottom and scooted down the first step.

Then he scooted down the second step.

By this time, his mother had made it to the garage to load the other two kids.

As I watched him scoot step by step, I was reminded of the steps all of us have to take in life. Just like my son, we have to take one step at a time.

We step at the rate and posture where we can maintain our balance, until we reach the end of the stairs.

If we move too fast or maintain too lofty of a posture, we will tumble down the stairs.

If we move too slow or stop moving altogether, we could get left behind or hold up the kid behind us.

Looking at all of the stairs at one time looks scary, focusing on one step at a time and conquering that step is not so scary.

My two-year-old like many adults, did not know the Father stood behind him lest he fall, nor did he realize that his mother would have waited for him to arrive.

Even though you are older than two, how are you moving along your stairs of life?

A MountainWings Original by James Bronner

The Dream
=========

It was an early Sunday morning before the sun was yet to make its presence known.

I dreamed.

The dream was vivid. A dream so real that when I awoke I knew it wasn't an ordinary dream.

I was in a church.

I was the Pastor of the church.

That isn't an unusual thing to dream since I am the Pastor of a church. The thing was, this wasn't my church.

I had never seen the building. There was a large crowd of people, I had never seen any of the faces. I was the Pastor, I was sure of it yet I was near the back of the church.

When the time for me to speak neared, I walked to the front. While standing, I placed my right hand on the wall just to lean against it.

The wall tore like thin newspaper. I was busy trying to put the wall back together but each time I tried to tape it up it just tore more. I gave up trying to fix the wall and just settled on delivering my sermon.

I woke up.

I had a very strong feeling that what I had just experienced was no ordinary dream. Many of you know the type. The dream clung to me like wet clothes, but I couldn't fathom it's meaning.

A church that I had never seen filled with unfamiliar faces with walls made out of paper?

What in the world did that mean?

I lay back in the still morning. The fresh air from the outside poured over me but the dream was still as dark a mystery as the night sky.

I drifted off and went back to sleep.

As I awoke and began preparation to go and minister to the church that I was familiar with and a congregation where I did know the faces, the light came on.

Not a physical light, but the light of understanding.

As if in an instant, like quick flash of lightning that lets you see your situation, I understood the dream perfectly. I understood what was being spiritually revealed.

It was a church with a location that I had never seen. It had a congregation that I had never seen. I sat near the back until I spoke. It had no walls.

It was MountainWings.

That dream was on July 29, 2001. MountainWings was much smaller. On that date MountainWings had approximately 38,000 subscribers.

A congregation of 38,000.

I would not recognize those 38,000 faces even if all 38,000 were assembled in one place.

I would not recognize the 38,000 but neither would the 38,000 recognize me. I sat near the back, just one of the crowd, unknown by face or name.

There are no walls with MountainWings.
No building, parking, rest rooms, or television cameras.

There have been so many of you who have written with the testimonies of how MountainWings has been the instrument that has given you the hope and inspiration to make it and become better. That's all a church is about.

Helping you to make it and become better.

That's a short sentence with a long meaning.

Helping you to make it and become better.
It boils down to that:

to help you make it here on earth.
to help you make it into heaven.
to help make you better, so that you can help make others better.

That's what it boils down to,

with or without walls.

Amen

The Moving Chair
= = = = = = = = = = = = = = =

"Daddy, my chair keeps moving!" my son exclaimed.

We were sitting in a small restaurant.
The chairs had wheels on them and sat on tiled flooring.

My son's chair was constantly sliding back and forth and side to side. It was annoying him. He couldn't stay in front of his plate without sliding the chair back into the proper spot.

"How do I stop this chair from moving?" he plaintively asked.

Was the floor slanted?
Was there vibration in the room causing the chair to move?
Was the floor slippery?

No.

I asked him, "Is Daddy's chair moving?"

"No," he answered.

"Do I have wheels on my chair?" I asked.

"Yes," he replied.

"Is my chair the same as yours on the same floor?"
I asked.

"Yes," he said.

"Daddy's chair isn't moving because Daddy isn't moving.
If you want your chair to stop moving...

...you've got to stop moving," I explained.

My son, like many kids his age,
has a hard time sitting still.

He likes to swing his legs back and forth, fidget, stretch,
twist, turn, and perform the many gyrations of the very
young.

We are like that.

Many of us have moving chairs that we are complaining
about.

It's not the chair.
It's not the floor.
It's not an earthquake.

It's not the boss.

It's not the church.
It's not the President.

It's not corporate America.
It's not the "other" person.
It's not society gone to pot.

In the vast majority of cases, we are moving our own chairs but blame the chair.

Just like my son, every problem that I have with things moving in the wrong direction, when I REALLY get quiet and honestly think about them, somewhere, at sometime, an action or inaction that I did started the thing to moving.

The first step to stopping anything from undesirably moving and shaking is to honestly see the real source of the problem.

Is your chair moving?

It's today, it's today!
=================

Those are the first words of the movie "Stuart Little."

It's a kiddie movie. I watched it with my two boys.

A little boy began the movie by running out of his bedroom shouting, "it's today, it's today."

He woke up his parents laying peacefully in their bed shouting, "it's today, it's today!" as he jumped gleefully around their bed.

The scene jumped to the three of them leaving the house as the little boy, George, exclaimed again, "it's today, it's today."

"It's always today," his mother remarked.

"I know, but this is today!" George replied.

Thus began a kiddie movie.

It's amazing how little it takes to fascinate a child. Such small things can make the world turn for a kid.

I remember my most enthralling possession.

It was a mini-bike.

You rarely see them now, but when I was a kid they were all the rage.

Basically, it was a very small scooter with a lawnmower engine on it.

Mine cost $175.00. It was a red Cyclops.

I paid every penny of it. My parents initially bought it, but I worked during the summer paying $25 a week for seven weeks on my newfound treasure.

I proudly showed my father the automotive type drum brakes on it.

He showed great interest.

I now know that he couldn't have given a hoot about the engineering of a boy's mini-bike, but thank goodness he didn't show it. I still remember his nodding head as I proudly explained it.

A childish thing can be remembered for a lifetime.

I remember the first night that I had it, my mother walked past my bedroom and asked, "What's that gasoline smell?" I had sneaked the mini-bike into the back door and had it parked in my bedroom. I was just that excited.

She made me put my prized possession in the basement.

I sometimes think about the mini-bike.

Not that I long for it, but to think that so little satisfies so much when you are so young.

I had to replace my car key recently. The key alone cost $175. Needless to say, I got no excitement from the key and though the car cost hundreds of times what the mini-bike cost, I got very little excitement from the car.

When we are young and uncluttered with the views of typical adulthood, everything holds a fascination.

The older we get, the more it takes and the shorter the excitement lasts.

Now we often wake up and say, "another day."

We could learn something from little George.

Little George was expecting wonderful things to happen to him because it's today. He was expecting to see wonders and miracles because it's today.

He was expecting to be thrilled, to be amused, to play, to see and learn something new because it's today.

You know what?

Little George was not disappointed.

Do you know what day it is?

It's today, it's today!

One Wish . . .

============

Recently I was talking to my brother about the one wish
God granted King Solomon in the Bible.

God told Solomon that he could have anything he wanted
just by asking, but he had only ONE wish.

My brother and I discussed with each other what that one
wish would be if we were allowed one.

Everything we came up with had some problem.

We knew that money and power were not the thing to
ask for because the rich fill the office of psychiatrists and
many take pills every day for depression. Money just
wasn't the answer.

We knew that revenge upon someone for something they
did was not a good choice because what goes around
comes around.

So we started thinking about higher things like
knowledge and wisdom.

We thought about it.

We had studied religion, science, business and health all
of our lives and there were a list of things that we knew
we should be doing but weren't. We needed greater
discipline more than greater knowledge and wisdom.

I said, "Maybe what we need is the ability to program ourselves like computers to do those things that we know are right." When we thought about this request it brought to mind a robot, for it does only what it is programmed to do, but it has no will to do otherwise and experiences neither pain nor joy.

Then we discussed spiritual gifts.

"What about the gift of prophecy?" I asked. This would help people know what path to take in life. Then we thought, if a man could see the future of anyone's life without error, that man would have no privacy. Everywhere he went people would be trying to find him, even at three in morning his phone would ring with people asking the question, "Can you see if my child is coming back home tonight?"

Even the ability to raise the dead has problems. Imagine if any corpse you prayed over would miraculously resuscitate to life.

Anytime someone died, people would call you or hunt you down for you to come and bring their loved one back to them.

Or what about just the ability to heal the sick without fail? If you had this, your peace would be lost to lines miles long from one hospital to the next waiting on a touch from you.

The answer to one simple wish contains a lot of information about the asker. It tells a lot about where you are and where you are going. After we discussed it long enough, we realized we had already been blessed with everything we needed. That which we didn't have, we had the ability to get.

The revelation that came to us was that what people really want the most is that which they spend most of their time trying to get.

If you only had one wish, what would you ask for?

What do you spend most of your time trying to get now?

A MountainWings Original by James Bronner

Victory
======

Muscles strained and veins popped as a determined frown spread across my face.

I put all of my manly strength forth.

The thing held fast, but I was determined that I would not be beaten.

Taking a deep breath, I lunged forward again, bending down and putting all of my 195 pounds behind it anew.

I trembled.

It trembled.

These are the times that vex a man's soul.

Manhood is at stake.

To fail now is the ultimate insult against all that is masculine.

Not me.

Not now.

I would not fail.

"Yield! Yield! Yield!" I secretly thought, hoping that my mental shout would somehow affect things.

I was almost outdone.

Almost out of energy as I felt both fatigue and pain set in.

With one last effort, summoning all within me, calling upon every last muscle cell, every ounce of will power, the inner strength that has carried countless men through such ordeals.

For all mankind I let a silent cry escape my lips in this last all or nothing attempt.

I felt it give!

Ever so slightly I felt its unyielding hold loosen.
I felt it open slightly and then I knew I had it.
I knew I had won.

There comes a surge of energy with the knowledge that you will not fail, that manhood will be preserved.

I had felt it give!

Spurred by the newfound confidence, I continued my relentless push.

With a loud "POP" it gave up, surrendering to the greater force.

I felt a sole drop of sweat travel down my left cheek.
That's OK, I had stood the test, met the challenge, and passed.

Exhausted but valiant, I leaned back in satisfaction.

I looked at my wife. She could see eons of primordial testosterone powered chest thumping in my eyes.

She was proud of her man.

With a smug look of confidence, I raised my hand with the evidence of my victory firmly encased within my grip.

She took the evidence of my triumph quietly acquiescing to the greater strength.

I leaned back again and smugly pondered the accomplishment.

To my shock she said, "One more time."

My left eyebrow raised slightly as I saw what my wife brought from behind her back.

I shuddered anew but concealed my anxiety with a masquerade of manly confidence.

I wondered silently,

"Why in the world do they make baby food jars so hard to open?"

For all the men who have had to open baby food jars in front of their wives.

You understand.

How Long?

= = = = = = = = = = =

I took my son to golf practice today.

The profoundly simple wisdom that comes from a child is amazing.

As he placed the ball on the tee and prepared to hit the ball onto the driving range, a lady watching my young son from behind asked him a question.

"How long have you been playing golf?" the lady asked.

"Since I started," my son quickly answered.

I chuckled at first but then a higher meaning came to light.

A MountainWings Moment.

I don't know whether more MountainWings Moments are coming into my world or whether I am just becoming more sensitive to the moments around me.
This was a MountainWings Moment.

A MountainWings Moment is a moment of insight that transcends everyday reasoning and takes your spirit above the ordinary.

He had no need to rack his brain trying to ascertain how many months or days he had been playing golf. At his age, he really doesn't comprehend months or even weeks. He lives in the present.

"Since I started."

That's exactly how long you've been a subscriber to MountainWings.

Since you started.

That's exactly how long you've been (fill in the blank).

Since you started.

"Therefore do not worry about tomorrow, for tomorrow will worry about itself. Each day has enough trouble of its own."

One of the world's greatest and most well known quotes tells you not to worry about tomorrow. That also applies to yesterday.

Most of our hurt and pain is because of the memory of yesterday or the fear of tomorrow.

In reality, my son had just begun playing golf when he placed the ball on the tee. He didn't care about all of the other times; he was playing now.

Today

Since he started.

When are you going to start living a fuller life?

When are you going to start experiencing the real joy of life?

When are you going to stop worrying about all of the things you can't do anything about anyway?

It doesn't matter how unhappy you've been.
It doesn't matter how long you've been feeling unworthy.
It doesn't matter how deep you think the damage is.

What matters is when you really start to see the light.

All that matters is the "since you started."

So when are you going to start. . .

Then with all of your negative history and the negative stuff, when someone asks you "how long have you been this happy?"

You know the answer to give them.

The Greatest Golfer In The World!

============================

"Who's the greatest golfer in the world?"

That's the question the golf instructor asked my son.

As I walked in the door, the golf instructor recognized me. He was the same instructor who taught golf to my late father.

He taught me.

I was bringing my son to be taught.

He looked at my son, not quite five, and asked him a question that anyone following the golf world would know.

He expected the universal answer.

One man has revolutionized the sport of golf. Virtually every major sport has dropped in participation while golf has skyrocketed. The rocket that has carried the sport upward is one young man.

The golf pro figured that my son should know that.

When we walked in the door, I explained that I wanted my son to take golf lessons. The instructor looked down at the little boy who barely reached my waist and asked the famous question.

"Who's the greatest golfer in the world?"

My son without blinking an eye or missing a beat instantly answered.

He knew without hesitation or doubt.

"My daddy," he answered.

The instructor smiled, understanding both the correctness and error of the answer.

I smiled, realizing the responsibility placed within my hands for the shaping of a young mind.

Do you realize to someone, especially if you have children, you are the greatest in the world?

YOU are the greatest influence, the greatest guide, and the one your children are most likely to imitate, not the celebrity.

Makes you feel like a Tiger doesn't it?

ONE

And One

========

I imagine everyone was expecting an issue about giving thanks on Thanksgiving Day. I deliberately didn't send such an issue.

Why?

Didn't you wake up TH8IS morning?

Can't you see this print NOW?

Don't you hear the sounds around you NOW?

Isn't your electricity on NOW?

Aren't you warm NOW?

Aren't you breathing NOW?

Won't you eat TODAY?

Thanksgiving Day is a great idea but it shouldn't be just a day, it should be an attitude.

I am more thankful for today than I was for yesterday. You see, I've got an "AND ONE."

Each year is "two thousand AND SOMETHING." 2003, 2004, 2005 ... Next year will be "two thousand AND SOMETHING PLUS ONE."

We have been granted one more year, an "AND ONE." Today is one more day than yesterday. It is an "AND ONE."

The breath you are taking now is one more than the last one.

We shouldn't wait until we are in our '90s to be thankful for each additional day. I am thankful for each of them now and especially the "AND ONE."

If you spend only one day a year giving thanks, you are missing out on 364 gifts a year.

We should have Complaining Day instead of Thanksgiving Day.

We should spend one day each year complaining and griping about the things wrong in our world. On that day we would complain about everything and everyone who we had problems with.

Halloween would be a good day for that. We could all turn into monsters for just one day instead of acting and feeling ugly most of the year.

Often, we spend 364 days a year complaining and one

day giving thanks. We should give thanks at least 364 days a year.

That's what I do now. I don't wait until Thanksgiving Day.

I have Thanksgiving all year long and I'm working on Halloween.

I'd like to get rid of the one unthankful day that I have.

Saying thanks each day does more than acknowledge the giver, it makes you realize the gift.

I give thanks now for tomorrow, for it will be even more of a miracle than today or yesterday.

So Happy Thanksgiving Day. Today!

This has been ANOTHER MountainWings Original,

an AND ONE.

When I Was Quiet

===============

"They didn't see me when I was quiet."

That's what my five-year-old son said.

I picked him up from school and as usual asked him how his day went. I often ask him what he did during the day.

"I got my name put on the board for talking," he said.

The teachers try to be strict about maintaining discipline. It's a good thing. Even though they can't use the paddle anymore as they did in my day, they do the best they can with the techniques that they are allowed to use.

If your name is on the board, you can't play during recess.

You can't get on the swings, the slide, or play any of the sports. If your name is on the board, you're grounded.

"I got my name on the board, but they didn't see me when I was quiet so I couldn't get it off."

Remember the last speeding ticket that you got?

They didn't see you when you were going slower and traveling at a reasonable speed. Down the hill and in a hurry and here come the blue lights. They didn't see you when you were quiet!

The boss catches you just when you dose for a second (well maybe longer than a second) after diligently working all day.

They didn't see you when you were quiet.

Your wife catches your eyes wandering as you admire the architecture of an elegant building that just happens to have a shapely female in front of it.

They didn't see you when you were quiet.

Why doesn't the world take into account all of the times that you were quiet? Why do you suffer so long for a moment's indiscretion?

How can a few minutes take an eternity to make up for?

Because of one of life's simple principles, it's a lot easier and faster to mess up than to clean up.
Harsh words uttered in five seconds can damage a relationship for five years.

All of us are still in school.
We still have teachers.
We still pass or fail tests.
There are still paddles in one form or another and there is still the board.

With many of the things in our lives, we simply need to slow down and be quiet.

That way we won't miss playtime.

A Little Dash
= = = = = = = = = = =

MountainWings   A MountainWings Moment
#1302   Wings Over The Mountains of Life

MountainWings used to be just plain text.

There were no dashes, just like the heading above.

Then a reader who is a graphics artist wrote in with a sample of what MountainWings could look like by just adding a few dashes.

The dashes didn't cost anything, they were no trouble to add, they didn't change the story, but they made it more pleasant to look at.

This is what the heading looks like now with dashes.

MountainWings   A MountainWings Moment
#1302   Wings Over The Mountains of Life

A Little Dash

= = = = = = = = = = = = =

Life is like that.

Every now and then, you need to add a little dash to life.
It won't change your story, but it will make it look a lot
better.

You can do it without much money; all it takes is a little
time and effort.

When was the last time you've gone to a play?
It's been that long huh?

Colleges have them, churches have them, there are many
groups that put on plays that are rather inexpensive to
attend.

Do you have a pet?
When was the last time you've gone to a dog or cat show?
It's been that long huh?

Most cities have them at least once a year. If you are on
the net, you can find when one is coming to your area.
If you like cats and dogs, you'll love the show.

When was the last time you've gone to a comedy club?
It's been that long huh?

Again, most cities have them. Find out when a comic
will perform who suits your style and go and laugh until
the tears fall.

When was the last time that you just sat in the park and listened to the birds sing and the soothing sounds of nature?

It's been that long huh?

There are a hundred other things that if you stop and think, you will realize that dashes are all around you each day.

Take a break and put a dash of spice in the everyday world.

Remember, on all of our tombstones will be the day we are born and the day we die. The only thing in-between - is a dash.

Time flies so fast as you age that years seem to dash by.

For little or no money and a small investment in time and effort, make the picture of life more pleasant to look at.

Add a dash. . .

My Mother's Job
===============

February 6.

It is a day that will always be burned in my mind.
It is the day my younger brother died at 38.

I wrote a MountainWings issue about that day,
The Big Flash, on page 119.

I developed a heart product from that day,
www.heartmiracle.com

I preached a sermon from that day that has helped many
with the loss of a loved one called "1 Hour and 40
Minutes." www.AirJesus.com

My mother never shed a tear. She said God showed her
life, not death. The revelation of the scripture, (Eccl 7:1)
"A good name is better than precious ointment; and the
day of death than the day of one's birth," became mani-
fest. It hurt, but she understood it.

She loved her son dearly as she loves all of her children,
as intense as any mother could, but she said, "My job is
done."

Her words echoed in my mind as I was in Florida on a
Friday night. My oldest son (five years old) had his first
basketball game on Saturday morning and I was going to
miss it.

I told him that I would be there for his second game and I wanted to be there for his first, but I was simply out of town and would not return in time.

There will be so many decisions that I will have to make with my children. That night, I decided to keep my "job description" clear.

Yes, I will train them to be successful in life.

Yes, I will make sure they are educated through college and beyond if they wish.

Yes, I will teach them the ways to keep their bodies healthy, their finances healthy, their families together, and how to have a good outlook on life.

I will do all of that, but the words of my mother's job ring strongly as my main job description.

My mother and father did all of the above to as near perfection as any child could ask, but it wasn't my mother's main job.

My mother said, "God gave me children, and it's my job to get them back to God. Though my son has left this life at only 38, I've done my job."

He left on Feb. 6, 2000, but on Dec. 31, 1999 he preached our watch night service at the church. His last sermon was entitled, "The Power of Love."

We often focus so much on the worldly things, material, educational, and status success. Those things are nice but they are just things, they are not the main thing.

My mother understood that. That's why of her remaining five sons, four of them are ordained ministers. One is founder and senior pastor of a church with over 6,000 members. One co-pastors a church, one is an assistant minister, and another pastors a church and is writing this issue.

I will be there to cheer my son in basketball at his remaining games, but I will understand that it is not the real game.

That is not what he must truly win.

My mother sat in the audience as my brother delivered the watch night sermon, smiling, with the knowledge that no matter what...

...she had done her job.

Ten Seconds

==========

You are right; it is the little things.

I was getting a special x-ray last week and the clerk put on my ID bracelet. She must have noticed I was nervous because as she put on my bracelet, she touched me with both hands and rubbed my arm.

She said something, but I don't remember what she said! I do remember, the touch... it has stayed with me for weeks now.

The above was a response to the issue, Itty-Bitty Things on page 257. It is amazing how such a simple thing can be remembered for so long. Think back on an act of kindness that you remember from long ago.

It was a dark morning in downtown Atlanta.

My father was a businessman, he had a store downtown, a wig and cosmetics store. He would take his sons downtown before school around 5:30 a.m. and we would pass out flyers to women hurrying to work.

I stood on a particular corner. I learned a lot about crowd psychology from those early cold downtown mornings. If there was a crowd of people coming across the crosswalk as the light changed, it was vital that you got the first person in the crowd to take one of your flyers.

If the first person took one, the rest would likely take one.

If the first person refused, the rest would likely refuse.

One morning a particularly rude lady brushed me aside with a rather mean look. That wasn't unusual and it is not her who I remember. The rest of the crowd following her across the street also refused my proffered circulars.

It was just a circular, and you get used to rejection when passing out circulars in the pre-dawn hours of a major city.

I don't remember the rude lady in front of the crowd.

I remember the last lady.

She was an older lady, perhaps mid-sixties to early seventies.

Her race was different from mine. Her hair was white with age and her frame frail from the years. She wore a black dress.

Did those things matter?

No, I just remember them.
She didn't need a wig and looked as if she never had nor would wear one. That I could plainly see.

Knowing the demeanor of the rest of the crowd, I made no real attempt to give her a circular; after all, she was the one person in the crowd who couldn't use what I was selling.

She stopped and extended her aged hand for one of my circulars.

I gladly gave her one and with that transfer, it lifted the rejection of countless others before her.

She spoke three words . . .

"Jesus loves you" and walked away.

That was 30 years ago.

It was an Itty-Bitty Thing that made a big difference.

Think on this:
What Itty-Bitty Thing made a big difference in your life?

Think also on this:
What Itty-Bitty Thing can you do to make a big difference in someone else's life?

Neither of the two examples above cost anything or took more than ten seconds.

Got ten seconds?

Pink and Blue Cows
================

I took my five-year-old son to visit his great grandmother, Ivestor. That's an unusual first name, but she's an unusual woman. She's 93 but that's another MountainWings issue.

This is about the trip home.

As I left her house in the country and prepared to get on the interstate, I noticed the traffic was nearly stopped. Evidently there was an accident or construction work that was slowing traffic to a crawl.

I decided to take the scenic, but slower, route home. It is a winding two-lane tour through the countryside.

I like to point things out to the five-year-old. He is very inquisitive, and I especially like to expose him to the wonders of nature.

He was fiddling with a plastic motorcycle in the back seat of the Jeep when I passed a farm with dozens of cows in the field.

I told him, "Look at the cows!"

He glanced up with his usual attentiveness to something different; the cows fascinated him.

"Are all cows black and white?" he asked.

The cows could have been poster cows for Gateway Computers; they were black and white with big patches of both colors just like on the Gateway commercials.

I replied with the expertise and wisdom of a scientist knowing many things about nature, "No, all cows are not black and white, cows come in all kinds of colors."

Children ask questions.

Some may seem silly, but underneath, they are pure scientific curiosity, the raw essence of wanting to know.

So my son asked me a question about cows from my statement.

"Do cows come in pink and blue?"

"Uhhh. . . no, they don't come in pink and blue."

"Do they come in orange and green?"

"Uhhh. . . no, they don't come in orange and green."

Suddenly all of my scientific wisdom seemed to be very stupid.

After all, I had told him that cows came in all kinds of colors.

Pink and blue, and orange and green does fit the category of ALL kinds of colors.

"Do cows come in purple and red?"
"Uhh. . . no."

After three attempts to find out if cows came in what obviously fit the category of "all kinds" of colors, my son either realized that his father maybe wasn't as smart as he thought or simply figured out an easier way to get the information he wanted.

He said, "Well, what colors DO they come in?"

My brain gears were already grinding. After the first two questions and my realization of my obvious blunder, I knew the questions weren't going to get any easier.

Hmmm. . .

Brown, yep, cows definitely came in brown. I had seen reddish brown cows but that was still brown. Black, white, and brown, those were the only cow colors that I could remember seeing.

My "all kinds" of colors was one additional color.

That was a MountainWings Moment.

Yes, just a simple question about cow colors and my grossly incorrect answer.

Children observe our words and deeds far closer than we may think.

They ask some good questions, whether expressed or not. Some we can't properly answer because we have given the wrong statement, either in words or action.

For the rest of the trip, I thought before I answered his questions. He kept asking questions about all types of things along the road.

A child's world is not limited by what we think we know. It is full of wonder and possibilities.
As we age, our bodies and imaginations, stiffen.

Pink and Blue cows?
No, they don't exist (at least I have never seen one).

If I had told my son that cows came in pink and blue, and orange and green, he would have believed me.

It's the impressionable and trusting nature of the child. It's the responsibility of the parent to lead the child to the best of his or her ability.

It's your responsibility to correctly lead anyone who trusts you and places you in a leadership position.

I learned a very valuable lesson today.

From a pink and blue cow. . .

The Hug

========

It was one of those mornings.
You know the type.

Things are tense.
Our infant son had been up all night.

My wife's eyes (along with the rest of her) were weary.
My oldest son, the five-year-old, wasn't feeling his best
either.

He was slow getting ready for school.
He understandably didn't feel like going.

It was just one of those mornings.
You know the type.

As I drove him to school, he was quiet.

When parents are tense and tired, the children feel it.
They know by word and gesture when their acts and
attitudes are less tolerated. After being fussed at, he was
sullen.

It was one of those mornings.
You know the type.

I walked him to his classroom as usual. He walked in,
removed his coat and hung it up. I usually give my son a
hug before I leave him in class.

I knew today he really needed a big hug, and maybe, so did I. He came forward with his arms outstretched. I bowed down, clasped my arms around him, closed my eyes and hugged him tight.

Normally, I would only hug him for two or three seconds but on this morning, I held him tight as the seconds ticked by like dashed lines on the highway.

All of a sudden, I felt him get heavier. Still clinging to my son, I opened my eyes. I understood why he had gotten heavier. His feet were off the ground. He had curled his legs up and his heels were only inches away from his backside.

He clung.
I clung.

Sometimes in life no words are needed.
The MountainWings Moment is stated in a feel and a fold. As he folded his legs up and trusted his father to carry all of his weight, he didn't get heavier to my spirit.

I actually felt lighter.

It was a ritual repeated countless times through countless years from countless parents to countless children.

The touch and embrace between a parent and a child make them both feel more secure.

It was one of those mornings.

You know the type.

Last
====

"I was in a beauty contest once.
I not only came in last, I was hit in the mouth by Miss Congeniality."
-- Phyllis Diller

We need the ability to laugh at ourselves sometimes instead of taking our shortcomings and failures so seriously.

Yes, you messed up with "_____."
Yes, your "_____" is not up to par.
Yes, if you could "_____" all over again you sure would do it differently.

Who do you know who hasn't messed up more than once?

If you have someone on the list of "never messed up," you just don't know him or her well enough.

We all do.
We all have.
We all will.

Yes, we should try to improve.
Yes, we should try to not make the same mistake twice.
Yes, we should keep the receipt on expensive lessons.

However, learn to laugh my friends.

Learn to laugh at yourself.

My wife often asks me, "why are you smiling or laughing at that?" when something unpleasant happens.

I respond, "And what good is frowning or fussing going to do?"

I tell her, "If a frown or fuss will make the situation one bit better, then I will frown AND fuss."

I keep smiling and laughing. Soon, she smiles.
Soon the situation isn't as bad as it first appeared.

Did the laugh change the situation? No.

It just changed the people in the situation.

So what if you came in last.

"But many who are first shall be last; and the last shall be first." (Matthew 19:30)

"The art of being happy lies in the power of extracting happiness from common things."
-- Henry Ward Beecher

Steamboat Bill

============

I often watch DVD movies on my notebook computer as I travel. I usually can't sleep on airplanes and it helps pass the time. My schedule stays so busy, it is often the only time I have to watch movies.

I use an online DVD rental service, I choose my DVD's and they mail them to me. When I finish watching them, I mail them back.

I had three DVD's with me as I left for a trip to Kansas. As I settled in my seat, I opened the envelope to see which one I would watch first. Inside were two comedies and "Steamboat Bill."

"Steamboat Bill?"

What in the world was that?

I didn't order any "Steamboat Bill!"

If you don't recognize the movie, "Steamboat Bill," don't feel like you are just so out of it that you don't know the latest movies. "Steamboat Bill" is not exactly a recent

movie. It was made in 1928.
I had never heard of "Steamboat Bill," so I couldn't have ordered it. I thought that they sent it by mistake.

I watched the one comedy on the trip to Kansas.
I watched half of another waiting in the terminal for the return trip and the last half on the way back to Atlanta. I still had an hour of movie watching time left when the second comedy ended.

I only had "Steamboat Bill," a movie that I didn't order.

Life often presents us with choices where we just have to choose the least unpleasant alternative. It was "Steamboat Bill" or nothing. I hadn't brought any books, I couldn't sleep, I was too tired after a long day to write, so it looked like "Steamboat Bill" and I had a date.

I popped it in the notebook and pressed, "Play."

The screen flickered like an old Charlie Chaplin movie. It was in black and white. The music came on and then the titles. The characters began speaking, or rather, their lips moved.

It was then that I realized this was a silent movie; the actors spoke no words that you could hear.

"How was I going to sit through this?" I wondered. A movie from 1928 with no talking people in it! How backwards could you get?

I watched an hour of "Steamboat Bill" on the plane. When the flight attendant said that it was time to turn off all electronics, I shuddered.

You see, I was totally wrapped up in "Steamboat Bill."

The movie was excellent. You would think that you wouldn't get much out of a movie with no talking. You would think that you needed all of the multi-million dollar stunts and sets to make a good movie.

"Steamboat Bill" had it all: action, mystery, suspense, compassion, treachery, and love.

All without saying a word.

I understood everything perfectly, or at least as well as any talking movie.

It was a MountainWings Moment.

I had often heard it said that most communication is on a non-verbal level. We speak more by gesture, facial expression, body language and tone than we do by the actual words.

I understood that after watching an hour of "Steamboat Bill."

It is not just what you say but more how you say it.

It was late when I arrived home. I had an early morning meeting. I am typing this MountainWings during a break in the day, but I can't wait until I get home from work.

I have to finish watching "Steamboat Bill."

"Steamboat Bill" has already taught me something.

I did not order "Steamboat Bill," but we don't order many of the lessons in life that we get.
The lessons are sent anyway.

The lesson of "Steamboat Bill":

1. Actions speak much louder than words.
2. What you do can speak so loud, people can't hear a word you're saying.
3. Don't think something isn't great because it's old.
4. Don't think something is great because it's new.
5. Silence is gold.
6. Gold isn't easily found.
7. Don't pre-judge.

If we learn the lessons well, we won't have to repeat them.

And that goes without saying.

The Birth of MountainWings

========================

For those who have asked about the origin of
MountainWings. . .

This is the story of how MountainWings.com came to be.

Although it's about MountainWings, there are similarities
to many of your lives. Read and Learn.

Where did the name MountainWings come from?

Someone else threw it away.

I subscribe to a service that sends a list of un-renewed
domain names. MountainWings.com is a domain name
just like Amazon.com, AOL.com, and Yahoo.com.
I invest in domain names as a side business.
I own a lot of them.

You register a domain name for a minimum period of one
year. It costs $15.00 per year on nameitright.com.

At the end of the number of years that you pay for, you are notified to pay again or else you lose the registration on the domain name and someone else can register it and own it.

That's what happened with MountainWings.com. Someone else owned the name but decided for whatever reason not to renew their registration and it showed up on the list. The list is long each week with hundreds of domain names on it.

When I saw the name MountainWings.com, something struck me about it. I just liked it. I had no idea what I would do with it, I just liked it. So I registered it.

Many of you feel that someone else has thrown you away just as MountainWings.com was thrown away.

We often feel rejected, dejected, unloved, and unwanted.

Within each of us is a treasure, un-mined gold and undiscovered value. Someone just has to be able to see the potential.

Someone else could see no value in MountainWings. You might say that they viewed it as dirt. I saw it as rich soil.

I kept MountainWings.com, but I didn't know what to do with it. I felt something about it; I just didn't know what. I didn't want to sell it. I even wanted to change my personal e-mail address to myname@mountainwings.com.

I just liked the name.

Many of you feel that way. There is something inside that you can feel bubbling with potential. You just don't know what.

You know that life has a great destiny for you, but you don't know which way to turn. You feel like I did with MountainWings, possessing something great but without direction or purpose.

Months after I had registered MountainWings, it still crossed my mind, but without direction and purpose I didn't know what to do.

Sound familiar?

I am a pastor of a church, a teacher if you will. Even though I teach people each week, I also need to be taught. So I found a teacher that I liked and could say that I wouldn't mind my life being like the external manifestation of his life.

That man is Pastor Wiley Jackson Jr., of Gospel Tabernacle.

I attend his Tuesday night services as often as I can. It's odd for a Pastor to attend another church. It may be odd but it's the right thing to do. Everyone needs to be taught and you learn more by listening than by speaking. So I go.

Pastor Wiley Jackson is in ministry with his younger brother, Rodney Jackson. I am in ministry with my younger brothers, C. Elijah and James. My brothers even write some of the MountainWings issues.
I chose a man who was doing what I wanted to do.

That's a basic principle. If you are going to follow someone, make sure they are where you want to go or at least going in that direction.

The main message was finished on this particular Tuesday night.

Minister Rodney Jackson had just delivered the message. He began talking. This was not in his planned sermon.

He said, "We should use all of the available resources of the world to reach people; we should be sending out e-mails every day."

MOUNTAINWINGS!!!

The thought instantly registered so strong on my spirit that it was like having a bucket of ice water dumped on my head.

I immediately went home and began working on it.
For two months I labored on the concept to make it happen.

What Rev. Rodney Jackson implanted into me that night was a seed.

A seed that was to grow in the dirt of the name that someone else threw away.

Thus, MountainWings, the daily e-mail, was born.
To make something good grow out of dirt always takes work.

Weeds grow without help, but good fruit takes work.

Several days ago I mentioned to Rodney Jackson how his seed had birthed MountainWings and six months after the birth over 10,000 people received it each day. Nine months later over 100,000 people receive "A MountainWings Moment" each day.

"I didn't mean anything that big, I had no concept of something of that magnitude," he said.

That's the power of a seed. You can't recognize mighty Oaks or giant Sequoia trees by looking at their seeds.

If the seed is never planted, watered, and watched over from weeds and predators, it will not grow into its destiny.

That holds true for your seeds implanted into your dirt.

You can have no fruit without seed.
Seed won't grow without dirt. Dirt won't yield to the seed without breaking it apart to make it ready.
The breaking apart is painful.

It's called plowing.
Dirt + seed + plowing + other factors = fruit.
The other factors are under divine control.
Rain, sun, and season are some of the other factors that are beyond our control.

For those of you who have e-mailed me to thank me for MountainWings and explained how it has helped and changed your lives, maybe you should tell the one who gave me the seed, the idea for MountainWings. Sure the idea came from God, but it came through a human vessel.

I don't know Rev. Rodney Jackson's e-mail address, only his mailing address.

It's a lot harder to write a letter compared to e-mail. It's almost a terrible drudgery. You have to print or write it, get an envelope, a stamp, then get to a mailbox.

That's okay though, difficulty is often a great sifter that separates the casual from the dedicated.

Your thanks are seeds to the seed giver. Most ministers also buy groceries for their families from your seeds.

You never know what you are imparting and what your thanks will grow into.

As with all things good, take it to The Third Level.

For those of you who have subscribed to MountainWings for months, hopefully you have learned that action speaks a lot louder than words and often it only takes a little action to say a lot.

His address:
Rev. Rodney Jackson, Gospel Tabernacle
277 Clifton St., Atlanta, Ga 30317

Why Me?
= = = = = = = =

This is an actual prayer request received on
MountainWings. Rarely do we publish prayer requests,
but this one touches in a special way.
It is unedited for correct English.

----

am ugandan girl aged 24. my parents died when i was 16.
my job today is to bring up my young siblings one boy &
three girls.

Now i know this is my responsibility but sometimes the
load is just too much for me that i break down and cry &
i ask God really why it had to be me.

Sometimes i think its' just too much for me to handle.
for instance the school begins next week and i... I loose
words sometimes.
I need your prayers pse

Why Me?

All of us have asked that question at one time or another. When the load gets heavy, the resources get thin, the hours of the day get longer and the sleep at night gets shorter.

We see others around us who have it so much easier. Or so we think. I have learned, never assume how easy the other person has it.

They may be wishing they were in your shoes, and the grass often looks greener on the other side.

I asked, "Why Me" once.

I received an answer from God. That answer is in the issue "To Whom Much Is Given" on page 247.

I sent the young girl in Uganda that issue.

Maybe it helped to shed some light on her "Why Me?" situation.

Maybe it will help to shed some light on yours.

Long before MountainWings, I answered an email from a woman who read my book, QuickFasting on the web, at www.QuickFasting.com.

For some reason, even though the book was about fasting, in a moment of despair she emailed me. She explained the situation that was causing her turmoil. Her husband worked long hours, the mothers in the neighborhood depended upon her to do so much with the children. So many people depended upon her that she was feeling overwhelmed.

I don't have my answer recorded, but I remember the gist of it.

I told her that she had a good hard working husband who was struggling to provide for the family. She wasn't concerned about him with another woman. He always came home sober and kind. He was there, just not as much as she wanted. I told her many other women dream of a faithful husband like that.

Children are a woman's most prized possession and most women are very particular about whom they entrust them to. Obviously, she had the trust and respect of her neighbors if they depended upon her so much and trusted her with their children.

They looked up to her.

If people constantly depend upon you, it means that you have something to offer. It usually means you have something they don't. It means that you are the giver and they are the recipient. It is more blessed to be on the giving end.

She emailed me back and thanked me profusely for changing her viewpoint. It made her see her life in an entirely different view, and she was much happier. Same life – different view.

Why you?

Just maybe you were chosen for a position of strength to help others.

Maybe you are the blessed one and you are meant to be a blessing to others.

That's Why You.

Because YOU can handle it.

The Waves
==========

Recently we were running short on e-mail capacity as we reached our subscriber limit. Now we are on an e-mail plan with more capacity and much excess. Such is life. . .

One moment you have a shortage. . .
The next you have excess. . .

One day you have nothing to do. . .
The next you don't have time to get it all done. . .

One day the refrigerator is empty and you are hungry. . .
The next you have a half eaten meal in front of you and you are stuffed. . .

One month you've got money to spare and you wonder what to buy. . .
The next you've got a bounced check. . .

One moment you are full of energy and can't go to sleep.
The next you are drained and can't get up. . .

One day you are the center of attention. . .
The next you wonder if anyone knows you are alive. . .

It's the waves of life.
They carry us up and down and all around.

Money, friends, your body, your relationships, your job,
and the rest of the list, they all vary. They all go in
waves.

It took me a while to really understand the statement,
"The Kingdom of Heaven is Within."

No commercial can show you that.

Commercials make you believe it's in the jazzy new car or
the big screen TV. Yes, those things can thrill you for a
moment, but it's only a wave. After a little while, the
thrill is gone.

I have always recognized that if money and things
brought happiness, then all rich people with things
would be happy.

It ain't so.

We easily see how poverty can cause unhappiness, but
we are deluded into believing that money solves all
things.

Life is full of stuff. I wouldn't trade my life with anyone,
it's one of the most blessed that I know, but it's still full
of stuff. One thing after another, one challenge after
another, one situation after another, day by day,
never-ending . . .

It's the waves and there is no stopping them from the outside. You can only calm the inside, so that like a submarine, you ride deep beneath the waves.

Though a storm is raging, you are at peace.

Most are tossed and turned by waves.
Some like the sub, ride deep beneath the daily storms in peace. Some simply surf the waves and have a lot of fun.

Some drown.

You can't stop the waves; it's the nature of the ocean of life.

You can only choose which method you will use to handle them.

You can be tossed like most.
You can drown like many.
You can surf and have fun while you can, but even a surfer gets tired and there's nowhere to sleep on a surfboard.

To ride comfortably beneath the waves requires a ship containing breath that is not our own.

That ship. . .

. . . is not crowded.

Peace - Be Still

PLEASE, I'M TRYING TO QUIT...

Weeds and Seeds

===============

This is not the typical inspirational or funny MountainWings; this is more educational and enlightening. It is something that will hopefully give you the knowledge and power to change, not just a quick good feeling.

This is an actual request sent to MountainWings.com

"PLEASE, I'M TRYING TO QUIT SMOKING, I HAVE DONE IT FOR 30 YEARS AND IT'S HARDER THAN I THOUGHT. MY HUSBAND SMOKES AND MOST OF THE FAMILY AND THEY ARE NOT MUCH HELP. I REALLY WANT TO QUIT. THANK YOU AND MAY GOD BLESS YOU."

Has there ever been something that your inner soul was quietly or loudly telling you to do? Smoking has mountains of evidence, articles, doctors, and advertisements telling you why you should quit. The real change has to come from the inside.

Cigarettes are a narcotic. Period.
They are the third most widely used addictive substance.

The third?

Yes, the third.
More people are addicted to the first two.

Did you know that chocolate contains ingredients that affect the brain in a similar manner as marijuana?

I quote from a research study: "scientists reported that cocoa contains anandamide, a pleasure-inducing compound produced in the brain, and 2-arachidonoylglycerol (2-AG) and Nacylethanolamines (NAEs), substances that further mimic marijuana by enhancing anandamide's effects."

The other of the top two is caffeine.   Simple coffee.

Notice the similarity of the source plants of cocaine, chocolate and coffee: coca, cocoa, and coffee.

If you want to know specific details, you can order the book: "From Chocolate to Morphine: Everything You Need to Know About Mind-Altering Drugs - The Newly revised authoritative source book covering substances from coffee to marijuana."

The majority of addictive drugs are in a chemical class called alkaloids. Just notice the "ine" sound in heroin, amphetamine, morphine, cocaine, caffeine, nicotine, etc.

I will try to keep the technical stuff short, but I was educated in chemistry before I became a Pastor and the writer of MountainWings.com. It sometimes helps to understand the science.

There is a graph that illustrates the relative dependence on various common addictive drugs at http://www.drugwarfacts.org/addictiv.htm

The facts state that cigarettes (nicotine) make you more dependant than heroin, and coffee makes you more dependant than marijuana.

You didn't know that cigarettes were more addictive than heroin and that coffee was more addicting than marijuana did you?

No, you didn't.

I say to the person who wrote that prayer request, MOST of us are addicted to something that we would be better off without.

Even Internet addiction has been compared to strong drugs.

The prayer request has five common elements with our addictions.

1. We want to change
2. We have been in the old habit for a long time.
3. It's hard to change.
4. Most people around us are unchanged.
5. We often need outside help or encouragement.

So how do you break an addiction to anything?

First, you need to understand what it is.

Look at the word – ADDICTION. ADD – I – C – TION

The word "Addiction" has five key words in it:

ADD – You have added something to your life. Anytime you add anything to life, it must fit into a space that is either empty or it has moved something else out of the way.

I – It's a personal thing. Regardless of those around you, it's always a personal thing and a personal choice.

C – You ADD things to your life only because you "SEE" them.
If it's unknown you can't see it.
If you can't see it you can't add it.

TION – This is a word ending that makes the root verb a thing.
Educate + tion = education, confuse + tion = confusion, relate + tion = relation, etc. When I ADD an addicting thing that I SEE, then I have an addicTION.

All addictions come from the "thing" filling a missing space. Often when people stop smoking, they start eating more. They gain weight because now they use food to fill the space the cigarettes filled. Overeating is another addiction, a big one.

If you really digest this, you will get the knowledge for a long lasting good feeling. You need this kind of thing, though it isn't as much fun to read. Forgive the length, even a surface treatment of the addictions in our lives is long.

Each of the five key words of "addiction" gives you a key to unlock and release you from the addictive thing in your life.

ADD – If your life is full, you won't need to add the addictive thing to it. A person doesn't drink to get full, they drink because they are empty. There is a difference. The addictive things attempt to fill an empty spot. Fill your life with good things, make it overflow, and there will be no room for the bad addictive thing.

I – It's still up to you. No matter what is going on in your world, you have the final say.

C – (SEE) Often you need to change your environment because what you see each day influences you. If you let your children run with other kids who do drugs, guess what? Your kids are far more likely to do what they SEE. So are you. If you change what you see, you will affect what you do.

Realize this, once you change, then YOU will become what others SEE and they may change because they SEE YOU. If your family smokes, then all that they SEE are smokers.

Suppose you quit? Now they can SEE a non-smoker. In all things there must be a first, why not you, why not now?

TION – Knowledge is great, but without acTION it is useless.

If you don't take the knowledge and use it, and make it a thing, the knowledge is null and void.

Realize that addiction is not a bad thing.
Addiction to a bad thing is a bad thing.

Some are addicted to truth, to helping others, or to the constant climb away from low thinking and low living.

See the thing; if it's a negative, subtract it from your life.
Only YOU can do it.

The fifth key word in addiction is "diction."
That's how you say something.
You have the final say.

Speak and believe that NOTHING of the earth controls you, especially not weeds and seeds.

Make it so.

Right now you know at least ten people who need to read this.

So what are you waiting for?

I hope that you understand the many meanings of that question.

Hole Ting
=========

Hole Ting

Hole Ting

Hole Ting

That's what my two-year-old says.

He has developed the habit of wanting it all.

My wife will often offer him a spoonful of food from her plate.

I will break off a piece of what I am eating and hand it to him.

He shakes his head.

He emphatically says, "Hole Ting."

He doesn't want a piece.

He doesn't want a spoonful.

He wants the whole thing.

I wondered, "Where did he get such behavior?"
Who taught him that?
Where did he pick it up?

Hole Ting?

Why didn't he want to share?
Why wasn't he satisfied with what was given to him?
Wasn't the piece sufficient?
The piece was plenty and he could get as many as he
could eat.

Why did he want the whole thing?

Was he acting like a child or an adult?

As I watched other children, I saw that it was more
innate for children to want the whole thing.
They wanted the whole toy without sharing.
They wanted all of mama's attention.
They wanted the swing or the tricycle all of the time.

Hole Ting

Many of the conflicts and wars are over the same thing.
People don't want to share.
They want it all.

Hole Ting

It's not just for kids anymore.

Sensitive

========

I bought an ultrasonic dog repeller.

It looks like a garage door opener remote control.
A red light glows when the button is pressed.

My wife, whom I affectionately call Puddin, is terrified of
dogs. This device would make it easier for her to walk in
the neighborhood without worrying about dogs. If a dog
comes close to her, she points the device at them and
presses the button.

The device emits an extremely high pitched and annoying
sound that humans can't hear, only dogs. It won't hurt
the dog but sounds like a loud siren to dogs and the
person can't hear it.

Ahhh, the power of technology. . .

We were leaving in the van with the two kids as I opened
the package. I proudly showed my wife the device and
explained how it worked.

I pressed the button to show her the light and to forever rid her of her fear of dogs bothering her in the neighborhood.

"Oww!" she said, "that thing makes too much noise."

"You can't hear this, only dogs can. It just psychological that you think you can hear it when you see the red light go on.

See, the kids didn't hear anything and neither did I," I said.

"But I can hear it, it makes a loud buzzing sound that hurts my ears," Puddin insisted.

We argued back and forth, I was trying to tell Puddin that she couldn't possibly hear it. The pitch was far too high for human ears. Neither of the boys, ages 2 and 5, could hear it and I couldn't hear a peep out of the device.

Being a scientist, I thought I would prove to Puddin once and for all that it was all in her head that she could hear the device. I took a sheet of paper and placed it over the device. Puddin would not be able to see the light when it turned on.

No light, no seeing me press the button, no psychological feeling of the buzzing, my point would be made.

I held the device under the paper and waited a considerable time. Then while Puddin's mind had drifted to other things I pressed the button.

"Oww!" Puddin hollered.

Puddin could hear the dog repeller!!!

What in the world?

This was not supposed to be, but it was irrefutable proof that she could hear what people were not supposed to hear.

That incident made me realize a phenomenon in the physical that also exists in the mental and spiritual.

Some people are simply far more sensitive to some things.

MountainWings goes out each day to over a million people. It is always interesting how a story that everyone else loves will strike one person in a totally negative way. For various reasons, there will be something that they are sensitive to that no one else can hear. Jokes are especially prone to this more than any other.

When they read the same issue that everyone else loves,

"Oww!!!"

MountainWings has taught me a lot about sensitivity.

There is much publicity about physical abuse. Battered wives and children fill our news reports. Yet, there are areas more sensitive than our flesh to abuse, the areas of emotions and spirit.

Words often hit harder than a fist.

385

We say things to others that we are not sensitive to, but they hear with a loud pain. Often, it is something that we say in fun, yet it knocks the wind out of the other person.

Like Puddin, you may not think they can hear a painful sound, but the sound hurts. The difference with words is that the pain doesn't stop when the words stop.

It can echo within the soul for years.

Relationships between spouses, parents and children, co-workers, even church folks, can be broken with a sound of harsh words that the sensitive hears.

Before you lash out at someone, blindly criticize them, or talk down to them, remember, they may hear in your words things that you cannot.

They may be sensitive; be careful when you press the button.

Inspiration
=========

A MountainWings sub-
scriber asked me, "Where do
you get your inspiration?"

That was
A MountainWings Moment.

Often a question can focus thoughts as you struggle to
direct your mind to provide the answer.

A simple and correct answer is that inspiration comes
from God.

Sure it does but He sends it through different paths.
The paths can be intense beauty, unbearable pain,
or anything in between. Both extremes inspire.

The word inspire consists of two words, "in" and "spire."
"Spire" is the peak or pinnacle of something.
"In" is just that.

Real inspiration comes from the God given ability (sent
through paths) to see the peak, the pinnacle, the best of
the thing, that either you are in or that's in you.

It's not all about a beautiful field of daffodils.
It's not all about a war torn battleground.

It's about you being able to see the best and the good of
the thing that you are in or that's in you.

MountainWings Moments have changed the way that I view things. The MountainWings Moments have not changed what happens, only the way that I view them.

I can get inspired now in so much. Those who write and say how much MountainWings blesses them inspires me. Those who write and say it's absolute nonsense inspires me.

One extreme lets you know how far you've traveled. The other extreme lets you know how far you have to go.

The road traveled and the road to travel are both inspiring.

As a MountainWings reader, you too will change. You will become the inspirer.

One day, maybe in the not too distant future, a co-worker, a relative, a congregation member, a friend, a child, will turn and ask someone close to them, "I wonder where they get their inspiration?"

It really won't be from MountainWings. MountainWings is just a path, not a destination.

It will be from within. That's where all God given paths eventually lead. To the kingdom of Heaven within.

The original meaning of inspiration was "to breathe in." Life is full of inspiration.

Breathe it in.

You Must Keep Going
=================

Sometimes you must keep going.

Life punches you in the stomach. It knocks your breath
out and leaves you bowed and gasping.

You lose a job. . . you must keep going.

You find out you have a serious illness. . .
you must keep going.

You have a headache. . . you must keep going.

Sometimes the things in life are not serious but they affect
you nevertheless. . . you must keep going.

You have a big argument with your spouse.
Neither of you feels like talking and maybe not even look-
ing at each other. . . you must keep going.
Your son rebels and you have a blowout with him. . .

you must keep going.

The bills seem to never end and the money seems to never start.

You must keep going.

There are times that make us just want to curl up, stick our heads in a hole, and make the world go away.

We can't because we must keep going.

Life is full of those circumstances.

Many of you when you woke up this morning, for a variety of reasons, didn't feel like getting out of bed, but you had to.

You must keep going.

In times like those, and we all have them, remember the blessing.

The blessing is not in that we must keep going.

The blessing is that we can.

Buzz Lightyear's Helmet

=====================

"See how Buzz Lightyear's helmet flips up! It is a working helmet," my five-year-old son excitedly explained.

He was sitting in the bathtub playing with an action figure called Buzz Lightyear from the movie "Toy Story."

I listened and watched intently as he explained every detail of the toy. It was about as exciting as mini-bike brakes.

In fact, it was exactly as exciting as mini-bike brakes. Over 30 years ago, I bought a brand new, candy apple red, 3.5 horsepower, Cyclops mini-bike for $175.00.

I worked during the summer and saved $25 per week for seven weeks to pay for it. I earned $1 per hour, so it took most of my pay to put $25 aside for the mini-bike.

If I could afford and purchased a multi-million dollar Lear Jet tomorrow, it wouldn't have half of the excitement that the Cyclops had. I remember that I rolled it inside of the house and parked it in my bedroom for the night.

My mother noticed the smell of gasoline in the house and asked what the smell was. When she discovered I had parked the mini-bike in my bedroom, she promptly made me take it to the garage. Nothing material has ever come close to the mini-bike in terms of raw excitement and the fulfillment of a dream.

So what does that have to do with Buzz Lightyear and his helmet? You see, the mini-bike had drum brakes, just like a car. The brakes weren't operated by hydraulics but rather by a cable from levers on the handlebars.

I remember proudly explaining to my father about the brakes on the Cyclops. How they operated just like his car. I explained how safe they were and the principle on which they worked.

My father listened as though I was explaining the secret of life to him. My father was not a mechanical man. I now know that he didn't really know what drum brakes were. He didn't care either, but I didn't know that. He knew that his son cared about them. He knew the importance of listening, even if it was something that he wasn't interested in.

I remember his intense steel gray eyes as they peered at the brake mechanism nodding approval. Drum brakes on the Cyclops, hinged helmet on Buzz, same thing.

It's been over 30 years. My father has been gone from this life nearly ten years. I still remember. The Cyclops is now nothing more than dust in some junkyard or landfill. The memory of the intense gaze and the nodding approval is still strong.

It's why I gazed so strongly and paid so much attention to the hinged helmet. Buzz, like the Cyclops, will soon be gone, but the memories will shape a spirit and remain.

Little things that you do can change a life.

You never know when that moment is.

What a person puts in front of you could be their dream and constant labor. You never know what a little attention can do.

You also never know what inattention can do.

My son was naked in more than the physical when he showed me Buzz. He had the shields removed and opened his heart to share what he held precious.

I thought that my father listened as though I was explaining the secret of life to him. I now realize that he was showing the secret of life to me.

Remember what is precious to another may not be to you, but it is precious nonetheless.

You'll have your opportunities to shape a spirit.

Don't let it pass you by, be it Buzz or brakes.

What grade are you in?
=====================

As I was taking my son to school he asked me,
"Daddy, do you go to school?"

The question hit me. I instantly recognized it was not a
simple answer. He then asked, punctuating my pensive
silence with another question, "Daddy, are you through
with school?" Both questions silenced me.

The answer on the child's level was obviously "No,
Daddy does not go to school because Daddy is finished
with school." That answer would have satisfied him and
would have been technically correct.

Writing MountainWings has subtly changed my thought
patterns. It would have satisfied my son, but it would
have left a lump in my throat.

A big lump that tasted like a lie.

Finished school? Not hardly!
I think I learn more now than ever.
I learn more now than I did in nursery, elementary, high
school and college. It's not so much that the classroom

has changed, but the student has changed. I now recognize the opportunity to learn through all of the experiences that life presents to us each day. I now recognize the benefit of that learning.

I still hadn't answered him as I steeped in these thoughts. Sensing a need to help his father understand the question, he said hoping to clarify his question, "school is a building." That also is very true.

School is a building of character, a building of knowledge, a building of wisdom and experience.

I think people and relationships have taught me more about communication than English 101. I think marriage has taught me more than Math 101 about what happens when you add one plus one. I think making ends meet each month has taught me more than Economics 101.

Reading, Righting and Rithmatic, the three R's, life's got them beat as far as learning is concerned. Especially Righting is difficult, if you understand the play on words.

My son would rather not go to school.
There are some lessons I sure don't want to repeat.

In life you can have two students with the same teacher, one will pay attention, learn the lesson, and pass the class with flying colors.

Another student will become distracted, focus on things other than the main purpose, lose interest, fail the class, and have to repeat it over and over. Many of the latter persuasion never pass but simply give up and move on, with the grade permanently on their record.

You have the same teacher, class and lesson but different students and results. Life is a school.

The simple words of a child plunged me so deep in thought. Were they really that simple?

Were they really the mere words of a child or a divine question sent through a child?

How did I finally answer my son?

"I sure am in school son, everyday, and I am not nearly finished, neither is my final grade tabulated."

What grade are you in?

One Voice
=========

My wife and I are away on a retreat.

We decided to go to the hotel gym for a workout.
The gym was ultramodern and we were the only ones
there. There were five TV's positioned over the
treadmills and exercycles.

She wanted to watch a cooking show.
I wanted to watch a sci-fi program.

She got on the last treadmill on the left, I got on the last
treadmill on the right and we both tuned to different
channels.

As we began to run, we both periodically got off the
treadmill to turn up the respective volumes on our TV's.

After a few minutes, both of our televisions were at full volume.

We had clear pictures but the cacophony of noise made it almost impossible to understand the story.

I now understood why all of the televisions were tuned to the same channel when we arrived. Too many voices cause you to misstep and not understand the story.

If you are running (or walking) alongside someone in life, the story will go a lot smoother if both of you have the same vision and hear the same sound. When you are on different channels you both get louder but hear less.

I turned my television off.

Cooking wasn't so bad.

After all, I would benefit from the meals.

Are you on the same channel as the one whom you have chosen to walk through life with?

Let those couples who have eyes see
...and who have ears hear.

Life's A Beach
============

The weather is beautiful. It is hot and sunny; the water must be cold. That's what I thought as I looked from my room onto the beach.

I was in Panama City Beach, Florida. I was on vacation. I took three days to get away alone and rest. The ocean is always a good place to go. It was a holiday weekend.

Hot summer holiday weekends are usually crowded in Panama City. The beautiful white beaches draw vacationers from around the world. As I looked out onto the beach from my room, the beach was nearly deserted, and there were only a few people in the water at noon.

My only explanation was that the water must have been freezing. That can sometimes happen with the ocean. It can be ninety degrees, and yet the ocean can be very cold. I had packed my wetsuit for just such an occasion. I usually swim for a long time and if the water is unusually cold, the wetsuit makes it comfortable.

I grabbed my stuff and headed to the beach. There was an eerie silence magnified by the lack of people.

I let my toes slide into the frothing surf as it crashed against the beach. I was expecting liquid ice. It was warm, very warm.

I waded out into the ocean, not worrying about bumping into anyone because no one was there. The ocean was beautiful. The water was crystal clear; it felt like a warm bath. It was perfect.

Why was I the only one in the water? The thought kept hounding me. This was peak season and a holiday to boot.

I swam until my muscles signaled enough exercise for the day. As I walked towards the beach with the surf crashing against my back, an old man walked out towards me. A woman whom I presumed to be his wife watched him from the shore. She shouted something that made me instantly realize why the sea was empty of people.

"Don't worry, I'll let you know if I see any sharks!" she hollered. That was it, the people were afraid of sharks, that's why the beach and the ocean were empty!

It was a MountainWings Moment.

I don't watch the news, but I knew about the recent sighting of sharks and the shark attacks off the coast. The fear has frightened an entire nation into staying away from the beach.

Listen to this lesson.

There are three levels in coming to the beach.

First Level - The Room.
There is a great benefit in coming to the ocean just to
hear the waves crashing all day and night. It soothes and
calms the soul. If I had not gone out on the beach,
I would have received a great benefit from being in an
oceanfront room, to hear the waves and to watch the sea.

Second Level - The Beach.
Lying in the sand and letting the sun bathe you in radiant
light is an experience. I usually never use a lounge chair,
I stretch out directly in the sand. I can use a lounge chair
in my back yard; at the ocean, I am a sand man.

Have you ever lain on the beach (in the sand) and tapped
on the sand? It rings like a wooden floor. I discovered
that today.

Third Level - The Ocean.
Did you know that ocean water is chemically almost identical to blood once you remove the red and white blood
cells? Three-fourths of the world is covered with water.
Three-fourths of your body is water.

The ocean is one of God's greatest natural creations.
So are you. I was tingling all over once I got out of the
ocean. So many missed the feeling because they were
afraid of being bitten by a shark.

Below are the top five biting injuries occurring in 1987 in
New York City:

Dog bites human	8,064
Human bites human	1,587
Cat bites human	802

Wild rat bites human   291
Squirrel bites human   95
1987 Shark injuries in U.S. 13

Am I belittling the few shark attacks and the traumatic death of the little boy who died as a result of a shark attack? Of course not, but all too often we let other incidents of the world block us from life.

I included the above figures to emphasize that although shark attacks do occur, they are overall very rare.

I asked the fellow at the desk about it.

"Yep, visitors are down because of the sharks, but the thing is, there has only been one shark attack and that was in another city a hundred miles away. Most of what people heard about happened on the Atlantic side and not on this side," he explained.

Here is another chart for 1996:
A Comparison with the Number of Injuries
Associated with Home-Improvement Equipment

Number of Injuries in 1996 from:
Nails, screws, tacks, and bolts 198,849
Ladders 138,894
Toilets 43,687
Pruning, trimming, edging 36,091
Chain saws 13,458
Pliers, wire cutters, and wrenches 15,957
Manual-cleaning equipment 14,386
Power grinders, buffers, and polishers 13,458
Buckets and pails 10,907

Room deodorizers and fresheners 2,599
Toilet-bowl products 1,567
Paints or varnish thinners 1,549
Shark injuries and deaths in U.S. 18

In 1996, you were over 2,000 times more likely to be hurt with your toilet than by a shark. Who would imagine that the water in your toilet bowl would pose more danger than all of the sharks, snakes, and other stuff in the ocean? Maybe since 1996 toilets have gotten a lot safer and oceans more dangerous, but I doubt it. I wondered, "How do you even get hurt with your toilet?" Those are the facts. That ought to put things in some perspective.

Fear causes so many of us to miss out on life and our destinies. The sharks not only kept people out of the water but out of the rooms with the beautiful view and off of the beach.

Understand this: THE FEAR OF THE SHARKS REACHED PLACES AND KEPT PEOPLE FROM PLACES WHERE THE SHARKS COULDN'T EVEN GO.

Fear will keep you off of all levels of enjoyment, even where there is little or no danger.

There are sharks in your world, some real, but most just magnified to the point where they paralyze us in our actions.

Did a friend or relative get bitten by the shark of love?
Did they get bitten by the shark of business failure?
Did they get bitten by the shark of divorce?
Did they get bitten by the shark of layoffs?

Did they get bitten by the shark of disease?
Did they get bitten by the shark of death?

Did their bites scare you so much that you won't go to the room, the beach, or the water?

I am typing on my laptop now as I look out on the ocean. The water is warmer than I ever remember. It is 2 p.m. The weather looks like something out of a tropical movie. Looking both ways I can see a mile of beach. There is not ONE person in the water.

I am not suggesting that you do stupid and risky things, but the things that hurt most of us are not the things that we fear. Cigarettes are the leading killer in the U.S. Cigarettes will kill more people in the time that it takes you to read this issue of MountainWings than sharks will kill all year, even with the increased shark activity.

When was the last time you've seen anyone scared of a cigarette? If you are going to be really scared of something, be scared of the terribly frightening things, the things that can destroy both body and soul. A shark can't do that.

Jesus put it this way, "don't be afraid of those who can kill the body but cannot kill the soul, rather, be afraid of the one that can destroy both body and soul. . ."

Wives hold back from their husbands because they are afraid that if they give him their all, he could one day leave, and they've given everything. Husbands hold back from their wives because they are afraid that if they love unconditionally, they may seem weak and lose control.

Both lose, and they lose a lot, because of fear. Sharks - where sharks can't even go.

Roosevelt said, "We have nothing to fear but fear itself." He knew what he was talking about. The world is full of sharks, but the biggest one of them all is the shark of FEAR. The shark of fear is not limited by the water.

So what would I have done if I had seen a shark fin? I would have exited the water most expeditiously, making quite a splash doing it. Then I would have stretched out on the beach, in the sand.

Go swim people, it's warmer than you think, and when you know the truth, there are not as many biting sharks as the world would lead you to believe.

Life really is a beach.

There is a room with a view, a beach, then a whole ocean awaiting you. Don't be afraid of the sharks.

Note: Days after I wrote this and first published it, a MountainWings subscriber sent a link with the actual shark attack statistics.

There were actually LESS shark attacks than the prior year but the ones that happened got more press. Know the truth...

Shark data Copyright International Shark Attack File Source of New York City biting injury data: New York City Health Department statistics quoted by U.P.I. (1982), A.P. (1986) and Newsday (1988)

Bloom Where You're Planted!

========================

In an effort to be cordial, I asked a certain young man how he was doing one day. Instead of hearing the common curt response of "Fine," he said,

"I feel like I have dug myself in a hole."

My response to him was, "The only place you start out on top is when you are digging a hole!" Immediately he retorted, "I didn't think I was digging a hole; I thought I was laying a foundation!"

Well, the truth of the matter is that everything is a matter of perception. Your outlook determines your outcome! It's better to be in a hole than in a rut.

A rut is simply a grave with both ends kicked out! The hole that this young man dug for himself was his foundation. This is a process of life.

You lose before you gain.
You give before you get.
You follow before you lead.
You establish a solid foundation before you build.
Before a farmer sows his fields, he first digs holes.
Every beautiful flower starts out as a seed in a hole.
Every fruit-bearing tree gets its start in a hole.

Most of us are in a hole of debt before we can graduate from college, but we don't have to stay there!

While digging a hole is dirty work and frustrating at times, it is necessary. Thomas Edison aptly stated, "Restlessness and discontent are the first necessities of progress."

So although being in a hole is confining and irritating, just hang on and learn to bloom where you are planted!

A pearl is formed in an oyster because of an irritant that enters. That irritant causes a secretion to be released, which actually forms the pearl. So, while you are irritated, realize that a valuable pearl is being formed deep within you.

Just keep your mouth closed, and bloom where you are planted!

Dr. Dale C. Bronner

The Bent Antenna
= = = = = = = = = = = = = = = = =

I have a six-year-old luxury
car that has given me nothing
but satisfaction since the day
I bought it. If it has given me any trouble, it was very
minor, and even better, it was covered by the warranty.
I would very highly recommend this model of vehicle to
anyone who's in the market for a virtually trouble-free car.

I know that it's improper to place too much value on
material possessions, so you will have to excuse me when
I tell you that I absolutely love this car.

It is very well kept, the interior leather is still very clean,
the mats are not soiled and dirty, it gets a hand wax job
every few months, and the engine still hums like a mock-
ingbird. I've had absolutely no complaints, until recently...

I was hurriedly leaving home early one sunny Saturday
morning. My haste resulted in some significant damage
being inflicted on my car. I didn't realize that my garage
door had only released half way.

As I backed out of the garage, I broke my antenna on the
incompletely opened garage door. There was enough
room for the entire car to go through, so it wasn't until I
was completely out of the garage that I saw that the door
hadn't opened all the way.

It was also at that moment that I realized that the loud

scrubbing noise I had ignored only a few seconds earlier was my antenna being attacked by the garage door.

My antenna was horribly mangled. What significant damage!! It may not seem significant, but it is.

The purpose of a car antenna is to receive radio signals. Without an antenna, no signal can be received.

Now, when my antenna goes up, it makes a very noisy, grinding sound. It sounds like a jackhammer trying to break up asphalt. It's as though the antenna takes on the same human-like stubbornness when someone is made to do something that he/she has no desire to accomplish.

When the antenna goes down, it's noisy. Again, it's displaying its resistance to perform the duty that it was designed to do. Not only that, it won't even completely retract so I end up driving around with a bent antenna.

Bent antennas and luxury cars are not a desirable combination. Once I saw the damage to my car antenna, it was easy for me to see how sometimes our built-in, innate antennas, our source of direction, can show the same signs of damage that my physical antenna suffered.

How's your antenna?

All of us have them, you know. Sometimes we refer to them as that "something" that "told me". It's that little nudge that makes you think twice when you're in doubt about something you are about to do.

Do you receive sound advice and guidance grudgingly and unwillingly?
Or do you welcome it cheerfully and happily, and then

act on it?
Do you go around bent out of shape?
Does even the slightest "scrub" totally disrupt your day?
Does friction from another source cause you to react with an equal, but opposite, reaction?
Or do you produce the same friction?

A bent, grudging, disobedient antenna is worse than no antenna at all. If I had completely severed my antenna, at least I wouldn't have to worry about its reluctance to extend and receive.

There would have been no signal to receive, and I could plead ignorance. But my bent, damaged antenna offers no excuses, because I can still hear all the radio stations. My antenna just doesn't make it easy for me to enjoy them.

As a result, I choose to keep the radio turned off altogether. That way I don't have to hear that irritating noise as the antenna reluctantly extends.

Does it take a while for your antenna to go up, when it should be active and receptive at all times?

Your antenna is always working, always willing to pick up the signal that offers the guidance that you're looking for.

That's what it's there for.
Learn to trust it.

A MountainWings Original by C. Elijah Bronner

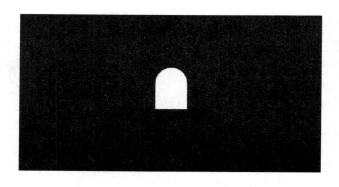

Crossing Over
= = = = = = = = = = = =

What a time for my life to end now?

The doctor announced that my time in this world was rapidly coming to an end. I only had a short while left.

I was happy, I was comfortable, I was just getting to a point where I could really enjoy things, and now this happens!

I have so much stuff that I barely have room to put anything else. My home has become crowded, I truly have been blessed and now I am asked to give all of this up?

I have too much to live for. I had it all. I was waited on hand and foot. My breakfast was brought to me in bed and even lunch and dinner if I wanted it.

I had someone to clean up after me too. I was the most important person around, a real big shot, and now this. I should have known it was too good to last. I had it too easy.

Everything was too perfect. I had no money worries, no job worries, my relationship was perfect. No woman ever loved a man as much as I was loved and now everything is changing.

Why?

Why can't things continue in perfect bliss?
Why can't God leave me alone and leave me happy?
Why do I have to endure pain and suffering?
Why do I have to die?

Why?

Pain is a good indicator that something is happening. That's why I was at the doctor in the first place.

The pain.

If you heard the screams, you would understand why I was upset.

The screams told a story that no medical report could ever say. The screams racked my entire body. I shook all over just from the screaming.

Have you ever yelled to the top of your voice?
Yelled so loud your throat became sore?
Yelled so loud your ears still echoed with your strained and pained voice?

That's what the screaming was like.
I can't even put in words how upset and lost I felt.

Have you ever had anyone describe to you what it's like to leave this world? I don't mean just passing away in your sleep, but to leave in the middle of pain and suffering.

Do you have any idea? I only had a short while left.

My lungs weren't working very well. They nearly weren't working at all. In these last stages they were filled with fluid. My digestive system wasn't able to process solid foods either. I was on a purely liquid diet fed through a tube. My eyes were very sensitive to light and my house had to be kept rather dark.

Suddenly another scream racked my body.

I only had a short while left.

The doctor's head shook from side to side in answer to pleas for more painkilling drugs. "We've done all we can for the pain," was the only answer.

I felt my time nearing as I struggled. I am a fighter, but there are some fights that you just can't win. Sometimes what you are fighting against is just too strong.

I struggled anyway.
It was all I could do and I wasn't going without a fight.

I saw blood.

The doctors say this is a sure sign that you have only

minutes left.
"So this is it," I thought.
I was too weak to fight it anymore.

I felt myself going down a long dark tunnel.
I saw a great bright white light at the other end.
I felt a strong force pulling me to the other side and a strong force pushing me out of this world.

What or who was waiting on the other end?
Faster than I thought possible, I was pulled through the tunnel.

I knew I had crossed over.

The light was overwhelming, a different kind of light.
Brighter by far than anything I had ever seen.

I looked back and there was a limp body on the bed that I couldn't even recognize. Was this the body that carried me through my old world?

I was in a different world, but was I dreaming, dead, or what?

I saw strange creatures like I had never seen.
They were big giants, but I felt surrounded by love.
Somehow, I knew that these strange creatures meant me no harm.

I heard them speak in a language that I had only heard through muffled dreams.

I heard the words…

"Here is your new son Mr. Bronner, would you like to cut the umbilical cord?"

This is my speculation on what my son Christian thought as he was being born on New Year's Day, the birth of a new year.

This is a different perspective on the miracle of birth. Read it again from the viewpoint of an unborn baby and you'll see a different meaning.

Birth is always painful and depending upon which side we are on, it can feel like we are dying, yet we are being born anew.

This is true for both natural and spiritual births.

We often go crying, kicking, and screaming into each new world, both those going

...and those left behind.

Each e-mail issue of MountainWings ends with:
Thank you for inviting MountainWings in your mailbox.
See you tomorrow.

Thank you for inviting these issues into your world.
Be Blessed, and maybe we'll see you tomorrow,
on MountainWings.com.